C000241822

The
Little Book
of the Sea

ALSO BY LORENZ SCHRÖTER

Skylarks and Scuttlebutts

The Little Book of the Sea

Food & Drink

LORENZ SCHRÖTER

translated from the German by ALAN BANCE

with additional material by SANDRA BANCE

Granta Publications, 12 Addison Avenue, London W11 4QR

First published in Great Britain by Granta Books 2009

Copyright © Lorenz Schröter 2007
Translation copyright © Alan Bance 2009
Additional material copyright © Sandra Bance 2009

Originally published in German as *Das Kulinarische Kielschwein*.

A CIP catalogue record for this book
is available from the British Library.

1 3 5 7 9 10 8 6 4 2

ISBN 978 1 84708 122 3

Printed and bound in the UK by CPI Mackays, Chatham ME5 8TD

What the world eats annually*

692 million tons† of
vegetables • 380 million tons of
fruit • 265 million tons of meat •
2 billion tons of cereal • 14 million tons of
algae • 143 million tons of fish catch—of
which 86 million tons are from marine fishing
including 10 million tons of crustaceans and
cephalopods and 5 million tons of mussels—
plus 9 million tons of fish from inland waters
and 48 million tons produced by fish
farms (both salt- and fresh water),
including 40% carp

*As of 2005 †1 US ton = 0.9 metric tonnes

Drunken prawns

～

Two dozen live prawns per person

Three pints Chinese rice wine (or sake)

Pour the rice wine into a large bowl and drop the prawns into it. Try to catch the merry little chaps with your chopsticks. The head should be bitten off first. Fun for the whole family.

The first restaurant review in the world

～

From the Epistulae of St. Theodore Studites

"In Galatea there is a village called Syceon…The postal road passes through the village, where there stands a roadside hostelry run by a very pretty girl called Maria, together with her sisters and her mother…In this house lived a god-fearing man called Stephanus, who knew how to cook the most excellent dishes. The ladies of the house had become respectful since giving up their profession of prostitution, and led a chaste and pious life. They devoted themselves to the art of cooking, entertaining governors and officers who congratulated Stephanus on his good food."

A milestone in the history of gastronomy—for the first time ever, an inn being praised for its food! The first restaurant critic was a saint, St Theodore Studites (758-826), the last great ecumenist of the Eastern Church, who took the side of the iconophiles in the Byzantine conflict of iconodules versus iconoclasts. He is celebrated by both the Greek Orthodox and Catholic Churches on the 11th and 12th of November, respectively.

From *A Narrative of the Mutiny on Board His Majesty's Ship Bounty* by William Bligh

*T*he quantity of provisions I found in the boat was 150 lb. of bread, 16 pieces of pork, each weighing 2 lbs, 6 quarts of rum, 6 bottles of wine, with 28 gallons of water and four empty barrecoes [casks].

After the mutiny on the *Bounty*, Bligh sailed off into the open sea, setting out from the volcanic island of Tofua, with 18 loyal men in an open boat 23 feet long. Tofua is part of present-day Tonga. Thanks to Bligh's superb seamanship, the castaways eventually arrived at Timor, in the Dutch East Indies, having travelled almost 4,000 miles. Not a single man was lost.

Bligh's mission on the *Bounty* had been to import breadfruit from Tahiti for cultivation in Jamaica, in the search for a new staple for the Caribbean plantation slaves. Food for the West Indies had previously come from North America, but the American Revolution ended the supply, and substitute provisions were needed. However, despite Bligh's success on his second breadfruit voyage, the slaves refused to eat breadfruit for about half a century, only using it to feed the hogs. It is now central to the Jamaican diet.

The fate of the *Bounty* and the mutineers who disappeared with her was a mystery until 1808, when an American sealer, the *Topaz* under Captain Mayhew Folger, accidentally came across Pitcairn Island—whose location was wrongly marked on the charts—and discovered the descendants of the *Bounty* rebels and the sole survivor of the mutiny, Alexander Smith. Folger's story was received without much interest in Britain, where the Tory London *Quarterly Review* commented sniffily that it had discounted the report until it had checked a few facts and found that the story tallied. It was just as well, because: "If this interesting relation rested solely on the faith that is due to Americans, with whom, we say it with regret, truth is not always considered as a moral obligation, we should hesitate in giving this publicity." Two British Navy ships, *HMS Briton* and *HMS Tagus*, came across the island in 1814, and found a model settlement. By then there was no thought of bringing Smith to justice. The news about the fate of the *Bounty* inspired a big hit on the London stage, a play called *Pitcairn*.

Who was Captain Birdseye?

The first actor to play Captain Birdseye in the famous fish finger advertisements was John Hewer (serving from 1967-1998: he died in March 2008, at age 86). He was succeeded by Thomas Pescod.

Civilizing the cannibals of New Zealand

A missionary reports in 1826:

"We never see human heads exhibited as formerly, nor do they, I believe, so frequently kill their slaves on the death of their relations…But when they are out at war I believe they are as barbarous as ever, killing and devouring those they subdue without any feeling of compassion."

(*Letters from the Bay of Islands: The Story of Marianne Williams*, ed. by Caroline Fitzgerald, 2004)

The best fish soup in the world

Serves four

1 lb. firm white fish, skinned (snapper, mullet, cod, sea bass)

3 teaspoons olive oil

2 large onions, sliced thin

1 leek, just the white part, finely chopped

4 cloves of garlic, chopped

1 bay leaf

1 pinch of marjoram

4 strands of saffron

1 teaspoon unwaxed orange zest, grated

1 dash white wine

1 lb. rough-chopped tomatoes

1 red pimiento, skinned, deseeded and rough chopped

2 tablespoons tomato purée

4 fl. oz. passata

16 fl. oz. fish stock

2 teaspoons brown sugar

3 tablespoons chopped parsley

salt and pepper

Gently heat the oil in a heavy saucepan. Add onions, leek, garlic, bay leaf and marjoram, cover and simmer for ten minutes, shaking pan slightly. Add zest, wine, pimiento and tomatoes and simmer for a further ten minutes. Put in passata, purée, fish stock, sugar, and saffron, and bring to a boil while stirring. Simmer for fifteen minutes on low heat without a lid. Meanwhile, cut fish into small chunks and simmer for eight minutes in the liquid. Season with salt and pepper and add half of the parsley. Remove bay leaf, serve soup in bowls and sprinkle with the rest of the parsley. Goes well with white bread and white wine.

Fish specialities available at McDonald's in various countries

~

Ebi-Chiki—prawn and chicken nugget burger, only in Japan

Shrimp Burger—prawns in bread roll, only in Korea

Fish McDipper—fish nuggets, only in Malaysia and Japan

McLobster—lobster burger, only in Maine,
and on the east Canadian seaboard.

Sea creatures with vitamins

~

Amount of daily requirement per 100 grams

Vitamin A
Eel 110%
Cod-liver oil 2,500%
Tuna 50%

Vitamin B1
Flounder 15%
Plaice 15%

Vitamin B2
Eel 19%
Mackerel 21%
Pollack (rock salmon) . . .21%

Niacin (Vitamin B3)
Salmon 42%
Mackerel 42%
Sardines 54%

Vitamin B5
Baltic herring 133%

Vitamin D2
Eel 230%
Eel (smoked) 1,800%
Buckling 620%
Herring 620%
Salmon 326%
Salmon (canned) 230%
Sardines 150%

Vitamin E
Herring 120%
Mackerel 120%

How to kill a lobster

~

Crustaceans and shellfish, apart from oysters, must only be killed by placing them in boiling water: the water must cover them completely and be brought back to a boil after they have been put in.

The exceptions are that:
1. Crabs may be killed by mechanically destroying the two main nerve centres; and
2. Shellfish may be killed by hot steam at over 100 degrees Celsius.

German Animal Protection Regulations, Para. 13, Section 8

Sea creatures with minerals

~

Amount of daily requirement per 100 grams

• **Iron**—oysters 50% • **Fluorite**—salmon 58%, herring 35%, mackerel 35%, flounder 20%, cod 20%, eel 16%
• **Iodine**—haddock 122%, pollack (rock salmon) 100%, prawns 655%, mussels 65%, cod 60%, mackerel 37%, herring 26%, halibut 26%, flounder 16%, salmon 16%, tuna 11%
• **Potassium**—stockfish (dried cod) 75%, trout 25%
• **Calcium**—oysters 8% • **Copper**—oysters 83%, lobster 23%, plaice 18% • **Magnesium**—prawns 20%, oysters 10%
• **Phosphorus**—salmon 20%, sardines 20%, whitefish 11%, pollack (rock salmon) 11% • **Zinc**—oysters 1067%, prawns 15%

Other ways to kill a lobster

Place the lobster in cold salt water, preferably seawater, and heat it slowly. A tip: add some seaweed. It makes the lobster taste even better. Rinse in cold water for a short while after cooking.

You can also drop your lobster into very cold water (just above freezing). When it has fallen into a coma, push an ice pick through its chest up to the head.

A lobster will also lose consciousness in a very high concentration of salt water. It may then not notice when it is dropped into boiling water.

It seems that another quick method of dispatch is to thrust a knife between the eyes, then cut the spinal cord.

The ignorant Spartan

"A Spartan was invited to a banquet at which sea urchins were served. He took one. He did not know how to eat it, and failed to notice his fellow diners' method. So he put the whole sea urchin in his mouth and tried to crunch it with his teeth. He found it hard going, as he couldn't crack the hard shell. He said: 'Damned fish! I'm not going to give up now, but it's the last one of these I ever eat!'"

This anecdote is told by Athenaeus, a Greek from Egypt who lived about 200 BC and recorded it for posterity in his book *The Deipnosophists and the Banquet of the Learned*. A deipnosophist is an accomplished dinner-table conversationalist, and the dialogues are very frank: alongside recipes for tuna, topics raised include the sexual preferences of gods, half-gods, and humans.

8

What is the right way to eat …?

Eel—May be—in fact must be—cut up with a normal knife, unless it is steamed, in which case use a fish knife.

Oysters—drizzle with lemon juice—really fresh molluscs will go on twitching! Using the sharp edge of the oyster fork, separate the flesh from the shell, and let the oyster slide down your throat. Some gourmets like to chew slightly before swallowing. Or you can spear the meat and drink the liquor afterwards.

Lobsters and langoustes—served split in half. Hold the crustacean by its tail and scrape the meat out with a fork. Gourmets break open the claws in the middle with lobster crackers and pry the meat out with a fork, or even with their fingers. Hors d'oeuvre cutlery is then used to eat the meat.

Caviar—eat directly from the jar with a spoon made of mother-of-pearl or horn, as metal spoons spoil the flavour. Russian millionaires like to have caviar spooned on to the back of their hand. Eat with blinis, toast or crème fraîche. The caviar should never, never be heaped on the toast!

Crayfish—twist the tail away from the body shell and crack the claws with the crayfish knife (that's the one with the hole in the blade). Pick the meat out with a twin-pointed crayfish fork. Eat it with a fish fork. Eating crayfish allows polite society to ignore all the classical rules of etiquette: you can break open the shell with fingers and teeth, suck out the meat and juice, and slurp it down. On such occasions it is best to use red tablecloths and napkins, as the crayfish juice will otherwise leave rather odd stains. This is one occasion when you should tie your napkin around your neck.

Mussels—take an open, empty mussel and scrape the meat out of the next one. For the first mussel, use a fork.

Sushi—There is a choice: you can use either your fingers or chopsticks, and you can eat the whole piece in one mouthful. Dip the rice into the little bowl of soy sauce provided. With good sushi, avoid overdoing the soy sauce or the wasabi (green horseradish), so as to preserve the special flavour of the fish. Start with the white, soft and mild sushi, and then graduate to the red, darker and stronger-tasting morsels. Eat slices of ginger in between, to cleanse your palate a little.

Household hints

In trout or sea bream, the eyes should protrude, and the scales should be shiny. To make sure the fish is fresh, push your finger into it: no depression should remain.

Fresh fish should be cooled down to a temperature between 0 and 1 degree Celsius (32–34°F).

Fish stays fresh longer when wrapped in cloth soaked in vinegar.

Using lemon with fish at one time served to mask the smell when it was less than fresh. But this is unnecessary with really fresh fish, particularly as the taste of lemon often overwhelms that of the fish.

Fish is easier to descale after it has been dipped in warm and then cold water.

Deep-frozen fish should be defrosted in the refrigerator. If it is placed in milk, the "frozen" taste disappears, and the aroma of the fish improves. The fish will also be more tender when cooked.

To cook fish evenly all over in the oven, put a medium-sized potato in its stomach so that it cannot roll over.

When frying fish, if you add some salt or lemon juice to the oil, the fish will not fall apart when you turn them over in the pan.

The aroma of fried trout, plaice, or herrings will be intensified by adding a little iodized salt to the pan.

If you slit fish fillets a couple of times with a knife they will not roll up when frying. Fried in oil or butter at medium heat, the fish will not dry out.

To remove the smell of fish, roll some marzipan between your hands, and then wash them in lukewarm water—the marzipan will absorb the fish smell.

A bowl of vinegar next to the oven will prevent fish smells from spreading through the whole house.

Bake a cake after cooking fish—helps to neutralize strong smells (this goes for paintwork and plumbing problems, too).

Chinese
fish dishes

~

Bawang bieji – farewell
my concubine · *Bilu haizhon-
bao* – jade green sea treasures ·
Gangshi bifeng tangchao xie – sweet
fried prawns · *Hong Kong style* – "fleeing
before the wind" · *Gongbao youyujuan* – rolled
squid palace-guard style (with peanuts) · *Lingnanfo
tiao qiang* – the Cantonese Buddha jumps over the wall ·
Longfeng jixiang – Dragon and phoenix bring good luck · *Meihua
guiyu* – plum blossom salmon · *Tianxiang baoyou* – heavenly scented
abalone · *Xiangbo songshu guiyu* – squirrel-mandarinfish with pineapple

What do they call the common mussel in …?

~

· German = miesmuschel · Russian = midiya
· Icelandic = kræklingur · English (alternative) = blue mussel
· Norwegian = blåskjell · Danish = blåmusling
· Finnish = sinisimpukka · French = moule commune
· Dutch = mossel · Spanish = mejillón
· Portuguese = mexilháo-vulgar · Serbo-Croat = dagnje
· Italian = mitilo · Japanese = murasakiigai · Polish = omulek
· Swedish = blåmussla

How paradise reached Europe

Sugar—The first crusaders discovered sugar-cane plants in Tripoli in Lebanon before 1100. Sugar was first recorded in England in 1099, and by 1319 it was noted that sugar was available in London at "two shillings to the pound", which would equate to about £30 per pound at today's prices. In literature, sugar was first mentioned by Wolfram von Eschenbach in his *Parzival*. After the discovery of the New World, the lucrative production of sugar cane in the West Indies called for intensive labor, which was supplied by the slave trade from Africa. The ports of Bristol and Liverpool acquired great wealth through sugar importing.

Cocoa—Columbus discovered cocoa plants in 1502 or 1512. Cortez brought the beans back to Spain in 1528, and from 1544 onwards in the Spanish court it was mixed with sugar and drunk as hot chocolate. Seventeenth-century European coffee houses also began selling hot chocolate. For example, it was served at the Queen's Lane Coffee House on High Street, Oxford, from 1656 and is still available there today. Samuel Pepys in his diary entry for 24 April 1661 mentions going out for a drink of "jocolatte" to settle his stomach— the morning after celebrating the coronation of Charles II.

Coffee—The first café was opened in Constantinople in 1475, but it was the British who led the European craze for coffee houses, with the first opening in Oxford in 1650, followed by London in 1652. One establishment favoured by city brokers eventually became the London Stock Exchange. Vienna acquired its first coffee house in 1683—while the city was still under siege by the Turks. The French had introduced cafés to the New World by 1715.

Cinnamon—was introduced to Europe by Vasco da Gama in 1502.

Tea—Tea was available in Moscow from 1618, and from 1650 in England. It was popularized thereafter in 1663 by the Portuguese wife of Charles II, Catherine of Braganza. But it was not until 1855 that tea was first grown outside China—in India.

Whiskey and rum streets

Because of their high concentration of bars or saloons, a number of roads have acquired the nickname "Whiskey Street". Others actually are Rum Streets:
Strönwei (in Kampen, on the Baltic island of Sylt)
Eastern Temple Street (Liuzhou, China)
Main Street (Salt Lake City, Utah)
Macdonnell Street (Guelph, Ontario, Canada)
4th Avenue South (Melrose, Minnesota)
Rum Street (Dallas, Texas)
Rum Jungle Street (Badung, Indonesia)
Al Ql Rum Street (Muscat, Oman)
Li-Rum Street (Taipei, Taiwan)

30 April 1789

From *A Narrative of the Mutiny on Board His Majesty's Ship Bounty* by William Bligh

At dawn of day I attempted to get to sea; but the wind and weather proved so bad, that I was glad to return to my former station; where, after issuing a morsel of bread and a spoonful of rum to each person, we landed … We came to a deep gully that led towards a mountain, near a volcano; and, as I conceived that in the rainy season very great torrents of water must pass through it, we hoped to find sufficient for our use remaining in some holes of the rocks; but, after all our search, the whole that we found was only nine gallons, in the course of the day …

Every person being returned by noon, I gave about an ounce of pork and two plantains to each, with half a glass of wine.

A fairly substantial prawn bun

Take about 40 pounds of prawns plus two monster pieces of bun made of flour, water and baking powder—each more than six feet in diameter and two feet thick. Put them together, and you have the biggest prawn sandwich in the world. Such at least was the claim made by its creator, the organizer of the Husum (North Sea, Germany) Crab Festival 2006.

A recipe for kokoda

Cubed fish steeped in lemon/lime juice, then squeezed and garnished with onions, chillies, shallots, grated carrots, and tomatoes, and combined with thick coconut cream. Usually served chilled.

Serves four

1lb. firm white fish	2 tomatoes, cut up small
3 lemons	green pepper
8 oz. coconut cream	salt
1 onion	1 chilli

Cube the raw fish and marinate in lemon juice in the refrigerator until its flesh becomes milky and opaque. Do not leave it too long in the fridge, or the fish will fall apart! Garnish with the coconut cream and the other ingredients, and serve chilled. This dish, pronounced ko-konda, originated in Fiji. But many coastal regions have their own version of raw fish marinaded in lemon juice. In the Philippines they make kilaw, where the marinaded fish is prepared in a green salad with garlic, turmeric, fresh coriander leaves and ginger. The Hawaiian poke involves shallots, spring onion, and roasted sesame seeds. The Ecuadorians pour off the lemon juice and make their cevice with orange juice, onions, garlic, olive oil, salt and pepper. Koy pa, the Cambodian variant, is made with tender raw beans, spring onions, chilli, garlic, and fish sauce. In Kenya they enjoy tilapia masala, over which they pour a hot sauce made of onions, tomatoes, garlic, chilli, garam masala, cumin, and red pepper.

Flotsam

Sylt, 16 March 2007—a school class found 25 kilos of cocaine.

Floridiana Beach, Florida, 11 December 2006—
two people out walking found 37 kilos of cocaine.

East End, Cayman Islands, 2 May 2006—
police collected together five kilos of cocaine.

Pirates' Beach, Galveston, Texas, 7 April 2006—
an off-duty policeman found a kilo of cocaine.

Basil Jones Beach, Belize, 9 February 1997—
a marine biologist found 113 kilos of cocaine.

Between Arcachon (France) and Bilbao (Spain), more than five
tons of cocaine have been washed ashore since January 2006.

But the beach at Puerto Capezas in Nicaragua is something
special: here you can find a packet of cocaine almost every day.

Seagull wine

Put the seagull in a bottle and fill it with water.
Seal the bottle carefully and place in full sunlight.
Allow gull to ferment. A drink that cheers up every igloo.

Tasty rotten fish

Gut and clean a Greenland Shark, and cut it into portions
of about two or three pounds. Bury it in gravel,
weigh it down with a slab of rock, and in
six to eight weeks (in summer)
or three months (in
winter) dig it up and
hang it out to dry
for four months. Cut
away the brown crust,
and serve the white flesh
with brennivin (Icelandic aquavit). Nowadays hákarl, the national
dish of Iceland, is produced in plastic
containers. Health warning: fresh Greenland Shark is poisonous, apart from the fins,
skin and liver. Because it has no kidneys, it has a
strong smell of ammonia. A similar but less time-
consuming process—needing only four weeks'
fermentation—is used to prepare rotten skate, which is
eaten at Christmas in Iceland. Japanese funazushi, related to
carp, is fermented for a year in brine, and then for four years in
rice. Swedish surströmming also uses the natural fermentation
process: Baltic herrings caught early in the year are topped,
heavily salted, and fermented in wooden barrels. Then
they are canned. Only when the can begins to
bulge from the fermentation will it be sent for
sale—traditionally from the third Thursday in August
onwards. The tins are so explosive that they must not be
transported by air. In Thailand, pla raa ("rotten fish" in
English) is prepared in much the same way.

Rotten Roman fish sauce

~

Uniformly popular throughout the Roman Empire was a terrifying sauce called garum, made from rotten fish. The exact recipe has been lost, but historians think it was made by mixing the blood and guts of salted fish with small whole fish such as anchovies, and leaving the mixture in a brine solution in the sun for two months. Vast quantities of this sauce, and a clarified version called liquamen, were produced, the latter particularly in Spain.

Although not cheap, it was used for everything from marinating

meat to flavouring porridge.
It is said that any Roman wreck explored on the bed of the
Mediterranean is likely to contain a cargo of garum,
and 60 per cent of a wrecked Spanish vessel's load from that time
will typically consist of garum or liquamen.

Anchovy

A small, herring-like fish, anchovy was to the ancient world what the herring became to the modern. It is still the basis for the finest fish sauce, and for the writer George Orwell's favourite toast spread, the wonderful fish paste called Patum Peperium or Gentlemen's Relish (from a nineteenth-century recipe). Anchovies are mentioned in Shakespeare. Falstaff in *Henry IV Part 1* is said to have run up a bill of 2s. 6d. (= half a crown, or twelve and a half pence) for "Anchovies and Sack after Supper".

The association between anchovies and drinking is reinforced by the 17th-century medical writer Tobias Venner, who clearly did not relish the fish, and wrote in his Via recta ad vitam longam ('the best manner of living for attaining to a long and healthfull life') of 1620:

"Anchova's, the famous meat of drunkards, and of them that desire to have their drink oblectate [delight] the pallat, doe nourish nothing at all, but a naughty cholericke blood ... and are therefore chiefly profitable for vintners."

Champagne from a sunken wreck

A bottle of 1907 vintage Heidsieck Monopole Goût Américain from the wreck of the Swedish schooner Jönköping was sold at auction by Christies' in 1998 for $4,068. In all, 3,000 bottles lay for 80 years 200 feet down on the seabed, at a constant temperature of about 4.5 degrees Celsius (40°F). The sugar content at 42.55 grams to the litre was as high as expected, and the alcohol content was 12.35%. About 200 bottles were bought by the firm of Caviar House. There are still a few available for sale today.

The last menu on the *Titanic*

~

The First Class service for dinner on 14 April 1912 offered:

*Shrimp canapés and raw oysters
with vodka, lemon and hot sauce*

Consommé or barley soup

Poached salmon with mousseline sauce

*A choice of Filet Mignon with foie gras
and black truffles or Chicken lyonnaise*

—OR—

Roast squab on watercress

Asparagus-champagne-saffron salad

*Minted lamb, Glazed roast duck or
Beef sirloin, served with potatoes,
mint tea timbales and creamed carrots*

—DESSERT—

Sorbet made from champagne, orange juice, and rum

*Chocolate éclairs, French vanilla ice cream
or jellied peaches, assorted fresh fruits
and cheeses*

Current wine list on *Queen Mary 2*

~

The list on the *Queen Mary 2* consists of
343 different labels of wine. Here is a small selection:

Red wine

Le Caprice Cabernet Sauvignon, France (house wine) $9.64 (£5.86)*

Hardy's "The Riddle", Shiraz Cabernet, Australia $13.75 (£8.37)

Chateau Julian, Bordeaux $14.75 (£8.98)

Rioja Crianza Tinto, Bodegas Marqués de Muclela $18.16 (£11.05)

Merlot-Cabernet delle Venezie Luna di Luna, Ca' Montini,
Italy $22.17 (£13.49)

White wine

Le Caprice Sauvignon Blanc, France (house wine) $8.64 (£5.26)

3 Hardy's "The Riddle", Colombard, Chardonnay, Australia $12.53 (£7.62)

Pinot Grigio del Veneto "Vita", Italy $14.10 (£8.58)

Kleine Zalze Bush Vines Chenin Blanc,
Stellenbosch, South Africa $15.42 (£9.38)

Veramonte Sauvignon Blanc, Winemaker's Selection,
Casablanca Valley, Chile $16 (£9.74)

Petit Chablis, J. Moreau et Fils, France $24.47 (£14.89)

*The conversion rate used throughout this book at the time of publication was $1.64 to £1; this rate is of course subject to fluctuation.

Captain's dinner

In the 19th century, steerage-class emigrants were obliged to supply their own food on the crossing to America. In an emergency (for example, if the voyage lasted longer than scheduled, or supplies were ruined), the Captain would dole out supplementary rations—the so-called Captain's dinner.

Today the Captain's dinner is a glittering gastronomic and social occasion, usually taking place near the beginning of a voyage. Invitations are much sought after. It helps if you occupy a state room, or if you are famous, rich, or a good-looking woman, such as Kim Novak, Scarlett Johansson, or Angelina Jolie. But some envious cruise passengers claim that the event leaves them cold: "I didn't pay all those bucks to eat with the help!" as the saying goes.

Provisions for a British sailing vessel in the 17th century

To supply a crew of 190 for three months

8,500 pounds of salt beef
3,000 pounds of salt pork
660 pounds of cod
20, 000 brown and white biscuits
30 bushels of oatmeal
40 bushels of dried peas
1 vat (30 gallons) flour
11 small vats of butter
11,000 gallons of beer
2 barrels of hard cider

1 May 1789

From *A Narrative of the Mutiny on Board His Majesty's Ship Bounty* by William Bligh

*B*y noon I had 30 of them [natives of Tofoa] about me, trading with the articles we were in want of: but I could only afford one ounce of pork, and a quarter of a bread-fruit, to each man for dinner, with half a pint of water; for I was fixed in not using any of the bread or water in the boat … At night I served a quarter of a bread-fruit and a cocoa-nut to each person for supper.

Fish diet—miscellaneous information

In contrast to the Neanderthals, Homo sapiens survived (according to British scientists) because their diet included fish, which made them more adaptable to varying conditions.

According to experts, fish is richer in Omega-3 fatty acids than olive oil.

A Berlin study based on a two-week fish diet showed that Omega-3 reduces blood pressure and combats heart disease.

There are reports from Sweden that oily fish reduces the risk of prostate cancer.

The journal *Archives of Neurology* tells us that eating fish wards off Alzheimer's disease.

An American study of African tribes claims that high fish consumption reduces appetite.

British research has established that a foetus will develop faster if the pregnant woman eats plenty of fish.

Other research in Sweden shows that living like a caveman on a stone-age diet of berries, nuts, lean meat, fish and vegetables reduces weight, trims the waistline, lowers blood pressure, and also dramatically reduces levels of a blood-clotting agent linked to heart attacks and strokes.

And finally: research in the Seychelles found that babies whose mothers are fish eaters are born with a raised level of mercury in their bloodstream.

PER CAPITA CONSUMPTION OF FISH IN KILOS PER YEAR 1995–1997, ACCORDING TO THE UNO FOOD & AGRICULTURE ORGANIZATION

Mongolia 0.1	Iceland 91
Germany 14	Tokelau Islands 152
Japan 66	Global 16

According to the NOAA (National Oceanic and Atmospheric Administration) Fisheries Service, per capita consumption of fish in the USA in 2006 was 16.5 lbs (approx. 7.5 kilos). This included a record 4.4 lbs. of prawns. "Of the total 16.5 pounds consumed per person, Americans consumed a record 12.3 pounds of fresh and frozen finfish and shellfish, up 0.7 pounds on the year before. Canned seafood consumption dropped 0.4 pounds to 3.9 pounds per capita. We consumed a record 5.2 pounds of fillets and steaks, up 0.2 pounds."

Bombay duck

~

Bombay duck is not a duck at all, but a marine lizardfish from southern Asia with a famously pungent odour. For export purposes, to create a gourmet delicacy for those who like strong flavours it is filetted, trimmed and cut into rectangular pieces, dipped in brine for a while, and then dried in the sun for about 40 hours. It is then pressed in a roller press and sun-dried for a further 10 hours. From 1997 to 2003, its importation was banned by the European Commission because it was not factory produced, but the ban was lifted once packaging took place in approved plants. Vacuum packed, where available it is fried quickly in restaurants to provide a crispy, almost anchovy-flavoured snack at the beginning of a meal. The etymology of the term is disputed, but the favourite story is that the smell reminded Europeans of the pungent odour of the Bombay (now Mumbai) Mail train in the monsoon season. The Hindi word for mail is "dak", hence Bombay dak or duck. Another version has it that the Victorians were embarrassed by the native name for the fish, "bummalo", because of its first three letters, and made up a name similar to "Digby chick", which refers to dried herring.

The price of lobster in restaurants around the world

~

GRILLED LOBSTER

Esplanade Mateus, S. Maria, Ilha do Sal, Cape Verde £17
Island Thyme Bistro, Salt Cay, Turks and Caicos Islands..........£26
The Green Parrot, Nassau, Bahamas (as a starter)........................£17
Tamnak Thai Restaurant, Port of Spain, Trinidad £23
Hotel Reykjavik Centrum, Reykjavik
(with oriental salad and risotto) £59

Restaurant NKong, Moscow
(with vegetables and Tonb-Katzu Sauce) £51

LOBSTER NEWBURG

Scoma's Restaurant, San Francisco £22

SOUTHERN ROCK LOBSTER

The Lighthouse Seafood Restaurant, Parramatta, Sydney £32

LOBSTER SALAD

Green's Restaurant and Oyster Bar, St. James's, London £45

The historical price of lobster

~

Per pound in San Francisco restaurants
(prices adjusted for inflation and rounded up or down)

1850	$3.50	(£2)
1875	$5	(£3)
1885	$7	(£4)
1900	$6-16	(£4–£10)
1910	$8-24	(£5–£15)
1920	$9-16	(£5–£10)
1930	$8-14	(£5–£9)
1940	$8-14	(£5–£9)
1958	$10-15	(£6–£9)
1968	$22-32	(£13–£20)
1980	$28-29	(£17–£18)
2000	$19-23	(£12–£14)
2006	$25	(£15)

The Queen vs. Dudley and Stephens
9 December 1884

"A man who, in order to escape death from hunger, kills another for the purpose of eating his flesh, is guilty of murder; although at the time of the act he is in such circumstances that he believes and has reasonable ground for believing that it affords the only chance of preserving his life."

At the trial of an indictment for murder it appeared, upon a special verdict, that the prisoners D. and S., seamen, and the deceased, a boy between seventeen and eighteen, were cast away in a storm on the high seas, and compelled to put into an open boat; that the boat was drifting on the ocean, and was probably more than 1,000 miles from land; that on the eighteenth day, when they had been seven days without food and five without water, D. proposed to S. that lots should be cast who should be put to death to save the rest, and that they afterwards thought it would be better to kill the boy that their lives should be saved; that on the twentieth day D., with the assent of S., killed the boy, and both D. and S. fed on his flesh for four days; that at the time of the act there was no sail in sight nor any reasonable prospect of relief; that under these circumstances there appeared to the prisoners every probability that unless they then or very soon fed upon the boy, or one of themselves, they would die of starvation.

Held, that upon these facts, there was no proof of any such necessity as could justify the prisoners in killing the boy, and they were guilty of murder.

Every basic law course in Britain and America features the case on which this 1884 verdict is based. In the same year, the two survivors from the yacht *Mignonette* were sentenced to death for murder, but Queen Victoria commuted their sentences to six months' imprisonment.

The mummy trade

Mum or mom is a Persian word for wax. It was adopted into Arabic, and acquired two different meanings: 1) "earth wax", signifying asphalt (or bitumen); and 2) preserved corpses. The Arabs presumably thought that the bodies of the ancient Egyptians were preserved in asphalt. From the Middle Ages onwards, mummy-powder or mumia was used as a medicine. Natural mumia was derived from asphalt, while artificial mummy-powder was produced by grinding down mummies. It was used to treat prolapsed wombs, blood clotting, epilepsy, rheumatism, toothache, intestinal complaints, lung disease, hair loss, broken bones, and consumption. After all, it was capable of keeping corpses in good condition for a very long time, so why should it not do the same for live bodies? Sodium salt of sulphonated shale oil and ammonium bituminosulphate, whose bituminous origins are indicated by their names, are still used in prescribed medicines, although sadly no longer under the picturesque name of mumia vera or "true mummy". It is known that mumia was in widespread use in Bavaria and Austria up until 1834. And as late as the 1970s a "witch" in New York is said to have obtained a mummy for medicinal purposes.

The price of mummies

Mumia was expensive, because the Arabs hid their ancestors to prevent them from being made into medicine by the Europeans.
In 1566, you could acquire a complete Egyptian mummy for 10 écus (French silver dollars).
In 1791, an ounce of mumia cost 1,000 German Taler (dollars).
In 1924, the German firm of Merck was asking 12 gold marks for a kilo of mumia vera aegyptica.

The rum list

In order of strength—low to high proof

Puerto Rico (world market leader); Cuba; Barbados; Trinidad; St Vincent; Guatemala (*Ron Zacapa* is regarded as the best rum in the world); Guyana; US Virgin Islands; Grenada; Jamaica

Ship's biscuit

Flour and water are mixed and baked, then dried out in a slow oven (i.e. baked again). The Romans called their double-baked panis nauticus ("sea bread") bis coctus, which eventually became our biscuit. Ship's biscuit, also known as hard tack or pilot bread, would be baked three or even four times, depending on the expected length of the voyage. It will keep practically for ever if not attacked by salt water, mice or weevils. However, if you value your teeth it is unwise to eat ship's biscuit without first dunking it in some liquid to soften it.

Sweet pea, olive oil and hamburgers

It was on 17 January 1929 that the strip cartoonist Elzie Crisler Segar let a pugnacious seaman loose upon the world: Popeye, the perpetual fiancé of Olive Oyl. Popeye's best friend is J. Wellington Wimpy, who has an insatiable appetite for hamburgers. Together with Ham Gravy and the Oyl family (Olive, her parents Cole and Nana Oyl, her brother Castor Oyl, and Uncle Lubry Kent Oyl), Popeye and Wimpy undergo all sorts of adventures. At some point Popeye adopts a noisy brat called Swee'pea, a combination of "weepy" and "sweet pea".

In Chicago in the 1930s, Eddie Gold opened a chain of hamburger restaurants called Wimpy, after Popeye's mate. The name survives in a number of so-called Wimpy bars in the UK today.

Popeye statues erected by deeply grateful spinach growers

Cristal City, Texas	Alma, Arkansas
Chester, Illinois	Universal Orlando Resort, Florida

How Popeye discovered spinach

Popeye's Greek ancestor Hercules originally gained his super-human strength from sniffing garlic. But his enemy, the evil Brutus, doused Hercules' garlic in chloroform and blew him into the middle of a spinach field—where Hercules, his mouth filled with the green stuff, discovered the vegetable's magic power!

—From the Popeye film *Greek Mirthology* (1954)

From *A Narrative of the Mutiny on Board His Majesty's Ship Bounty* by William Bligh

he beach was now lined with the natives, and we heard nothing but the knocking of stones together, which they had in each hand. I knew very well this was the sign of an attack. It being now noon, I served a cocoa-nut and a bread-fruit to each person for dinner … We were now sailing along the west side of the island Tofoa, and my mind was employed in considering what was best to be done, when I was solicited by all hands to take them towards home: and, when I told them no hopes of relief for us remained, but what I might find at New Holland, until I came to Timor, a distance of full 1200 leagues … they all agreed to live on one ounce of bread, and a quarter of a pint of water, per day … Our stock of provisions consisted of about one hundred and fifty pounds of bread, twenty-eight gallons of water, twenty pounds of pork, three bottles of wine, and five quarts of rum. The difference between this and the quantity we had on leaving the ship, was principally owing to loss in the bustle and confusion of the attack. A few cocoa-nuts were in the boat, and some bread-fruit, but the latter was trampled to pieces.

Lobscouse

~

Serves up to six

½ lb. of braising steak
½ lb. neck of lamb
2 onions
4 large carrots
5 lbs. potatoes
2 meat stock cubes
1 dessertspoon sunflower oil
dash of Worcestershire sauce
salt and pepper

Cube the meat and brown in the oil to seal. Season lightly with salt, pepper and Worcestershire sauce. Rough-chop the onions, slice the carrots, and cut about a third of the potatoes into small cubes. Place the meat in a saucepan half filled with cold water; cover the meat with onions, then carrots, then potatoes. Sprinkle the stock cubes on top, heat the pan and simmer gently for up to 2 hours, stirring regularly. When the sauce is thick and the onion is breaking up, add the rest of the potatoes, adjust seasoning, and again simmer gently for a further 2 hours until the pot is ready to serve. It tastes even better the next day.

This stew was a favourite with sailors, and was brought to Liverpool by Northern European seamen. In time, Liverpool sailors acquired the nickname "scouser", which today applies to everybody from Liverpool. It is a name they are proud to bear.

The tastiest fish from ...

~

- Thailand (Issan)—salt fish
- Canada—king salmon (chinnock)
- Spain (Asturia)—kokotxas, cheek of cod or hake
- Barbados—flying fish
- Senegal—fish yassa
- Japan—lung of fugu, or puffer fish
- USA—shad
- France—top fillet of angler fish

American shad in trouble—or are they?

~

Shad are an anadromous marine fish, which means that they ascend from the sea each spring up rivers to spawn. Shad fishing has a long history as one of the oldest traditional industries of the North American coasts. Overall, American shad are said to be threatened. They must be released immediately when caught. (Although hickory shad, a close relative, may be creeled.) According to scientists, in the Susquehanna River the shad population dropped by more than 90 per cent over the seven years up to 2008. Remarkably, the threat is nothing new. The *New York Times* in January 1884 reported from New Haven, Connecticut: "The State Fish Commissioners express the opinion that the present modes of fishing in the Connecticut River are so destructive as to threaten the speedy extermination of the shad, and in their annual report they call upon the Legislature to investigate the matter of the pollution of the rivers and streams of the State by refuse matter from mills and factories."

On the other hand, American shad have returned to central Virginia for the first time in a century, thanks to the successful release of shad fingerlings in the Rivanna River. In Maryland, students from schools throughout the Potomac River watershed recently helped restore the American shad to the Potomac. They discovered that the Little Falls Dam was the problem, and they overcame it by creating a fishway or fish ladder that enabled the shad to continue their journey upriver. The students are now cleaning up streams and rivers in their own neighbourhoods. (See Sandy Burk's book from 2005, *Let the River Run Silver Again!*)

Ciguatera—the best fish poisoning of all

*A*bout 50,000 people worldwide suffer from ciguatera poisoning every year. You get it by eating fish from tropical waters: tang, barracuda, grouper, wrasse, moray, parrot-fish, carangid, red snapper, tuna, bonito, or mackerel. These predatory and reef-dwelling fish are ciguatoxic: they consume toxic single-cell organisms. Kira Achaibar et al. tell us in an article in *Practical Neurology* (2007) that: "The ciguatoxins are a family of heat-stable, lipid-soluble cyclic polyether compounds that bind to and open voltage-sensitive Na+ channels at resting membrane potential, resulting in neural hyperexcitability, as well as swelling of the nodes of Ranvier." Wow! Not bad for a "primitive" dinoflagellate. There is no antidote. All you can do is pump the stomach, induce vomiting, take laxatives, and pray.

Ten favourite fish dishes in the UK

Other than fish & chips (see below)!

1. Deep fried whitebait
2. Dressed crab
3. Fisherman's pie
4. Fish cakes
5. Fish finger sandwiches
6. Jellied eels
7. Kedgeree
8. Kippers
9. Potted shrimps
10. Scampi and chips

Fish & Chips

250 MILLION portions of fish and chips were sold in the United Kingdom in 2006. A quarter of all white fish consumed there was served over the chip-shop counter—i.e. 60,000 tons.

Ten percent of all potatoes consumed consist of chips—500,000 tons in all.

Altogether there are 11,500 fish and chip shops in Britain, compared with the 1,250 branches McDonald's now has.

5 May 1789

From *A Narrative of the Mutiny on Board His Majesty's Ship Bounty* by William Bligh

*O*ur supper, breakfast, and dinner, consisted of a quarter of a pint of cocoa-nut milk, and the meat, which did not exceed two ounces to each person: it was received very contentedly, but we suffered great drought. I dared not to land, as we had no arms, and were less capable to defend ourselves than we were at Tofoa … To our great joy we hooked a fish, but we were miserably disappointed by its being lost in getting into the boat.

The best Chinese restaurants with Michelin stars

Hakkasan	London	8 Hanway Place	Tel: 0207 927 7000
Sichuan Food	Amsterdam	Reguliersdwarsstraat 35	Tel: +31 202 269327
Chen	Paris	15 Rue du Théatre	Tel: +33 145 79 3434
Wing Lei*	Las Vegas	3131 Las Vegas Boulevard	Tel: +001 702-770-3388

*The only Chinese restaurant in North America with a Michelin star, as of 2008

The best kitchen knives

~

According to Masoyishi "Masa" Takayama, who runs the super-expensive Masa Restaurant in New York

Shun Classic (Japan) \ Misono Ux 10 (Japan) \ Korin Vg Silver (Japan) \ Mac Superior (Japan) \ Wüsthof (Germany) \ Global G 7 (Japan) \ Oxo Good Grips Pro (Japan) \ Wolfgang Puck Hohlschliff (USA) \ Zwilling J. A. Henckels Twin Cuisine Santoku Knife (Germany) \

McDonald's Filet-O-Fish

~

400 calories
Total fat 28% * 8g sugar
40 mg cholesterol (13%)
640 mg sodium (26%) * 1 g dietary fibre (5%)
0 mg Vitamin C (0%)

Too late!

~

François Vatel was the most famous chef of the 17th century. The feast he created for Nicolas Fouquet, Louis XIV's finance minister and the richest man in France, was the undoing of his master; it was simply too luxurious, and led the King to throw Fouquet into jail in a fit of jealousy. Vatel was a Swiss-German whose name was actually Watel, and he invented the famous Crème Chantilly (crème fraîche, sugar and vanilla). But in 1671, as maître d'hôtel organizing a very large-scale dinner for Louis XIV, he was mortified when the fish he had ordered did not arrive in time, and felt so disgraced that he committed suicide. The main account we have of the event is that of Madame de Sévigné, although she was not actually present herself:

Madame de Sévigné in Paris to Madame de Grignan
(her daughter-in-law) in Grignan, Provence, Friday, 24 April 1671:

> "But here's what I learned while arriving here, which I can't get over, and I don't know what else to do but to talk to you about it: in short, it's that Vatel, the great Vatel, "maître d'hôtel" of Monsieur Fouquet, and currently that of the Prince, this man capable beyond all others, whose good sense was able to support all the care of a State, this man that I knew … you see at 8 o'clock this morning the fish delivery hadn't arrived, he wasn't able to endure the humiliation that he saw coming on himself, and to make a story short, he stabbed himself. You can imagine the horrible disorder that such an accident caused to the festivities. And imagine that the fish delivery arrived, perhaps even while he was in the process of dying."

Nelson's blood

Lord Nelson was brought home to London from the Battle of Trafalgar in 1805 victorious, but dead. His body was placed in a barrel of rum to preserve it during the long journey. The story goes that when the ship arrived in London, Nelson was still there but almost all the rum was gone. The jack tars had "broached the Admiral" and tapped into the barrel. Since then, rum has also been known as "Nelson's blood".

And a bottle of rum!

Oh, a drop of Nelson's blood wouldn't
    do us any harm
Oh, a drop of Nelson's blood wouldn't
    do us any harm

Oh, a drop of Nelson's blood
    wouldn't do us any harm
And we'll all hang on behind.
So we'll roll the old chariot along
An' we'll roll the golden chariot along.
So we'll roll the old chariot along
An' we'll all hang on behind!

[The next two verses begin with:
"Oh, a plate of Irish stew wouldn't do us any harm" and
"Oh, a nice fat cook wouldn't do us any harm".]

Yo-ho-ho and another bottle of rum!
Fifteen men on the dead man's chest
Yo-ho-ho and a bottle of rum!
Drink and the Devil had done for the rest
Yo-ho-ho and a bottle of rum.

Dead Man's Chest?

If you have ever wondered what fifteen men were doing on a dead man's chest, it seems to be a tale of castaways. Quentin van Marle tells it in the *Geographical Journal*, published by the Royal Geographical Society:

> "In the early 1700s, the pirate Edward Teach—known as 'Blackbeard'—punished a mutinous crew by marooning them on Dead Man's Chest, an island 250 yards square surrounded by high cliffs and without water or landing places. Each was given a cutlass and a bottle of rum, and Teach's hope was that they would kill each other. But when he returned at the end of 30 days he found that 15 had survived."

Dead Man's Chest belongs to the British Virgin Islands in the Caribbean. Van Marle was himself marooned on the island for a while when his scuba-diving boat broke down. He found there was no food there. It was occupied by pelicans, lizards, non-poisonous snakes, and mosquitoes.

Modern piracy

The most dangerous strip of sea in the world is the Indian Ocean off Somalia. Pirates armed with AK-47s and rocket-propelled grenades made 31 attacks on shipping there in 2007, and by May 2008 there had already been 23 attacks. Until five years ago, a ship was reasonably safe if it put 50 miles between itself and the Somali coast, but now even 200 miles is not enough. (A country's "Exclusive Economic Zone", where it has sole rights to marine and mineral resources, extends 200 nautical miles out to sea.) Captured ships are released for a hefty ransom, and their high earnings allow the pirates to buy faster boats and more sophisticated GPS systems. A gunman on a pirate ship typically earns between £6,000 and £18,000 a year, a fortune in Somali terms.

Pirates and fisheries protection

Some see Somali piracy as a rational economic activity in a lawless country. There has been no functioning government in Somalia since the early 1990s. Its coastline is 1,880 miles long, the longest in Africa, and scores of European and Asian fishing boats trawl illicitly in Somali waters, running big risks for high returns. At any one time there are about 500 foreign-registered boats fishing in Somali waters, the Europeans boats catching tuna or prawns, and the Asian ones going for shark fins.

The Somali pirates are skilled, and sometimes call themselves "marines", claiming to protect their country's resources from foreign exploitation. The crews of boats they attack are seldom harmed. This is a truly global arena. Combined European and US naval units patrol the area (though this has merely obliged the pirates to move further north). The financiers behind the pirate attacks are based in the UAE, Kenya, or even Canada, London, or Hong Kong; they can earn a return of several million pounds on a single strike.

If the illegal fishing stopped, then so would the piracy. There is some truth in the pirates' claim to be acting as a kind of irregular coastguard. Ransom payments are regarded almost as legitimate fines by both pirates and ship owners.

Rum and the revolution

~

Rum was not just the demon beverage of pirates, slavers, buccaneers and, as one historian put it, "all the vagabonds who scoured the New World".

New research tells us that the part played by rum in developing North America and launching the America Revolution has been overlooked, partly because Prohibition made sure it was written out of the history books. The somewhat barren Northeast USA did not produce enough grain to make whiskey. New Englanders traded cod and timber for molasses from the West Indies to make into rum. The colonists drank a lot of their own rum, but also sold some of the surplus to the Indians. The results were catastrophic. To quote Benjamin Franklin: "… indeed if it be the design of Providence to extirpate these Savages in order to make room for cultivators of the earth, it seems not improbable that Rum may be the appointed means. It has already annihilated all the tribes who formerly inhabited the Sea-Coast." But rum was also bartered for slaves from West Africa, with equally devastating results there.

The vicious triangle

The rum trade was triangular. The rum that was made from the molasses
that had been traded for cod was then bartered in West Africa for yet
more slaves destined for the sugar-cane plantations of the Caribbean, or for southern mainland colonies. (George Washington
sold an uncooperative slave in the West Indies for a barrel
of rum, among other things. He ordered rum for
his troops, and was very fond of it himself …
something airbrushed out of the historical
picture since Prohibition.) The trade was
the dynamo driving the economies
of the New England and other
North American colonies,
in contrast to the sluggish
French-Canadian or
Spanish ones.

Drinking with the enemy

Problems arose when the New England colonists could not get molasses from the British colonies in the Caribbean, who used it to make their own—apparently superior—rum. So they turned to the French islands, which had a "molasses lake" because the Paris government would not let them make rum, out of fear of competition for French wine and brandy. The result was that the North American colonists traded with the French throughout the wars being fought against the French for the survival of the English-speaking American colonies.

Not unreasonably, perhaps, the British thought that the colonists should help to defray the costs of a war that had been fought to protect them, and the Navy was given the job of collecting tax on molasses. The Admiralty was inclined to be tough on the colonial merchants who had so recently traded with the French enemy. Deep resentment was generated, and that was how rum became the essential issue of the Revolution: the real "spirit of '76"!

(See Ian Williams: *Rum: A Social and Sociable History*)

44

Alcohol rations

The Captain General of Flanders, Philipp von Kleve (1456-1528), allowed his crew a daily beer ration of about half a gallon per sailor. His fleet carried more beer than water—seven and a half times as much—as Philipp meticulously noted in his campaign records.

In 1588 Spanish seamen were issued with half an *azumbre* (about one and a half pints) of sherry or wine per day. The Armada had about 12,500 gallons of water on board, and about 18,000 gallons of wine.

The Swedish ship *Vasa*, which sank on its maiden voyage, carried about half a gallon of beer per man/day.

From 1655 until 1 August 1970 every sailor in the British Navy received a tot of rum. Latterly, this amounted to half a pint of rum at 50 proof. In 1776 every British matelot was issued with a gallon of small beer (1% alcohol) and half a pint of rum daily.

Grog and flip

The first two cocktails ever were invented at sea

The British Vice-Admiral Edward Vernon (1684-1757), victor of the Battle of Porto Bello, had a name as a reformer. He opposed press-ganging and campaigned against drunkenness on board ship. He gave orders for the daily rum ration to be watered down. Because he always wore a coat made of grogram (gros grain, a mixture of wool and silk), which he had rubberized to make it more or less waterproof, his nickname was "Old Grogram". Too much of Old Grogram's grog could make a sailor "groggy". A popular song of the time praises the Admiral's innovation:

> *A mighty bowl on deck he drew*
> *And filled it to the brink;*

Such drank the Burford's gallant crew
And such the Gods shall drink;
The sacred robe which Vernon wore
Was drenched with the same;
And hence its virtues guard our shore
And Grog derives its name.

But, sadly, the Navy continued to be plagued by drunkenness until Victorian times, despite Vernon's reforms.

Flip

The beer dispensed on board ship was very low in alcohol: only one to one and a half per cent. So in the early 18th century, seamen started adding spices and brandy to it. A sailor who had drunk too much "flip" felt capable of jumping right over the mast; hence "to flip".

Among the Maoris

"Soon after we landed we meet with 2 or 3 of the Natives who not long before must have been regaling themselves upon human flesh, for I got from one of them the bone of the Fore arm of a Man or Woman which was quite fresh, and the flesh had been but lately picked off, which they told us they had eat; they gave us to understand that but a few days before they had taken, Kill'd, and Eat a Boats Crew of their Enemies or strangers, for I believe they look upon all strangers as Enemies."

—*The Journals of Captain Cook*, written by James Cook during his voyage with the *Endeavour* (1768-1771).

Aquavit Linie

*O*n 1805, a ship carrying Norwegian aquavit (a potato-based spirit, about 60 proof, flavoured with caraway and other spices) sailed to Indonesia in the hope of selling it there. Failing to find any buyers, however, the captain took his cargo back to Norway. When the barrels were opened, the flavour was found to be vastly improved. It had been stored in old oak sherry barrels and acquired a new taste as well as a richer colour, and the constant movement at sea appeared to have refined the spirit. Aquavit Linie is still transported twice across the equator, making the round trip to Australia. It seems no amount of shaking on dry land can produce the same result. If you look through the bottle, on the back of the Aquavit Linie label you can read the name of the ship, the date, and the route it took.

Prairie Oyster

Singapore has its Singapore Gin Sling, Brazil its Caipirinha, New York its Manhattan Cocktail. Even Germany has its own recipe for Prairie Oyster, known as a hangover cure in slightly different versions around the world:

> 1/2 of a glass of tomato juice * 1 egg yolk *
> 1 teaspoonful of lemon juice * 1 teaspoonful of
> olive oil * 2-3 teaspoonfuls of Tabasco * 1 dash
> of salt * 1 dash of pepper * 1 dash of paprika

Swill the olive oil around in the glass. Add the tomato juice, lemon juice, Tabasco, salt and pepper, and stir. Stir in the egg yolk and sprinkle with paprika. Some people add a shot of brandy. Other recipes stress that the egg yolk should remain intact.

The best fish chefs

Here they are: the winners in the fish category of the most prestigious international cooking competition, the Bocuse d'Or. All the chefs competing had five hours to prepare their dish, and they all cooked the same fish.

2007—Sven Erik Renaa from Norway—Norwegian halibut
2005—Jonas Dahlbom from Sweden—Icelandic angler fish
2003—Donal Loriaux from Belgium—Norwegian fjord trout

The UK's top ten fish & chip shops

The shortlist for the 21st national Fish & Chip Shop of the Year competition, as reported in The Times *on 13 January 2009*

1. Anstruther Fish Bar & Restaurant (Fife)
2. Finnegan's, Porthcawl (Wales)
3. The Fish & Chicken Inn, Ballymena (Northern Ireland)
4. Colman's of South Shields (Tyne & Wear)
5. Thornton Fisheries, Thornton Cleveleys (Lancashire)
6. Merchant Fish Bar, Bewdley (Worcestershire)
7. Petrou Brothers, Chatteris (Cambridgeshire)
8. Scooby Snax, Brightlingsea, Colchester (Essex)
9. The Plaice, Winchester (Hampshire)
10. Daniels Fish & Chips, Weymouth (Dorset)

Thousand Island dressing

The name makes it sound like some exotic concoction from the South Pacific, but the origins of this popular salad dressing, often used with prawns, are much closer to home. It is made from mayonnaise and chilli sauce (peppers and tomatoes), plus finely chopped pickles, onions, and hard-boiled eggs. The Thousand Islands are on the St Lawrence River in upstate New York. However, there are conflicting stories about how the dressing originated. It certainly dates from the early 20th century, and one popular legend has it that George Boldt, owner of the Waldorf-Astoria hotel in New York, was cruising his yacht amongst the 1,000 islands of the St Lawrence on his way to Boldt Castle on Heart Island, which he owned. His steward prepared lunch, but discovered he lacked certain ingredients he normally used in his dressings. He extemporized with the ingredients he had to hand, and George Boldt was so impressed that he ordered it to be served at the Waldorf. The steward rose to fame as Oscar of the Waldorf.

A different version has it that the dressing was invented by a fishing guide, George LaLonde, who ran an inn with his wife at Clayton, NY, in the Thousand Islands region. The couple served "shore dinners" to customers after their day's fishing, presenting their unusual salad dressing. On one occasion, LaLonde guided a famous stage actress, May Irwin. She loved the dressing, and is said to have given it its name. Asking for the recipe, she handed it on to her friend George Boldt, who requested his famous maître, Oscar Tschirky, to introduce it at the Waldorf. He was given the credit for having invented Thousand Island dressing.

Hangtown fry

Hangtown was an early name for Placerville, California, where this dish is said to have originated. It is a kind of omelette (some say hash) involving eggs, bacon, and oysters, and there are two different stories about its origins, not completely incompatible with each other. Many accounts hold that during the days of the gold rush a miner who had struck it rich strode into the El Dorado Hotel (now the Carly House Hotel) and demanded the most expensive dish they could produce. Both eggs and oysters were costly and hard to come by at the time. The other story is that outlaws sentenced to death—in a town famous for hangings—could postpone execution for a while longer by requesting "hangtown fry" for their last meal. It could take a few days for the ingredients to be assembled.

It is quite possible that condemned men had heard about the expensive dish invented for the lucky miner, and requested it to delay their execution—if their wishes were respected.

Rat-free islands

Madagascar • Amrum • Lively Island, Falklands • Campbell and Kapiti, New Zealand • Sangalaki, Indonesia • Lundy, UK • Kure and Tern, Hawaii • Norfolk Islands, Australia

Rats leave sinking ship

There are two types of rat, both originating in Asia, which have spread to every continent. Rattus rattus is the black rat, also known as the roof rat, and the other is the larger brown rat (Rattus norvegicus), also known as the sewer rat, water rat, and Norway rat. Black rats love attics, while brown rats are keen on cellars and sewers. Experts argue about when and how the black rat made its way to Europe. Was it 2,000 years ago (it appears in ancient Greek images), or did it come during the Crusades, or perhaps not until the great age of discovery, when it may have travelled on the explorers' ships and carried the plague? On the other hand, it is universally agreed that the brown rat conquered Europe and every other continent (except Antarctica) in the 18th century. It comes from the steppes of central Asia, and is not comfortable in forests or in the cold. The black rat, however, came from the forests of south-east Asia, and is better at adjusting to a harsh climate. In the 1990s it was on the red list of endangered species drawn up by the IUCN (International Union for Conservation of Nature). Nowadays, though, its numbers are healthy once more.

In south-east Asia rats were often taken along in canoes as live food stock. Since they could not swim from island to island, the DNA of their descendants still living there can tell us what corner of Asia settlers on various South Sea islands originated from some 3,500 years ago.

Islands and coasts named after commodities

~

Spice Islands
Nutmeg and cloves come from the Molucca Islands, Indonesia

Coffee Bay, South Africa
A ship that ran aground there in 1863 lost its cargo,
and some of the beans took root.

Tobago, Caribbean
The name derives from the Haitian word tumbaku—tobacco!

Islands and countries that have given their name to food and drink

~

Kafa—coffee comes from this Ethiopian province.

Mokka—after al Mukha in the Yemen; it was from here that
coffee was distributed around the world.

Bourbon (Vanilla)—sometimes called Bourbon-Madagascar
vanilla. Vanilla originally came from Mexico, but today
most vanilla is produced by Madagascar and Réunion
Island. Réunion was formerly known as Île Bourbon,
hence Bourbon vanilla. The island was renamed after the
fall of the Bourbons, and the name "Réunion" celebrates
the joining up or union of revolutionaries from
Marseilles with those in Paris in 1792.

Bourbon (Whiskey)—As France had supported the American
independence movement, a few districts in the US
adopted French names: Lafayette, Louisville, Versailles—
and Bourbon in Kentucky, where whiskey was later
distilled.

Spice Islands

Tabasco is produced exclusively on Avery Island, which is not really an island, but a salt dome in Louisiana, 2 ½ miles wide and 3 miles long.

Nutmeg originally grew only on the Banda Islands (southeastern Moluccas).

Real cinnamon comes only from Sri Lanka

Islands with food or drink names

Sandwich Islands—This was the original name given by Captain James Cook to what is now Hawaii (not to be confused with the South Sandwich Islands, the mostly uninhabited British dependency in the South Atlantic Ocean), after his sponsor, John Montagu, fourth Earl of Sandwich. Cook was killed in the Sandwich Islands/Hawaii in 1779. Some years later the sandwich snack was also named after Lord Sandwich, who is said to have invented it to eat at the gaming table, so that play would not be interrupted.

Parsley Island—Spain and Morocco are in dispute over possession of Isla del Perejil. The island may in fact have been named after a certain Perez Gil, rather than the pot-herb.

Muscat—nothing to do with the muscat grape or wine variety. The Greeks gave this name to what is today the capital of Oman. The name of the grape derives from the French word musc, "musk".

Mark Twain on European coffee

~

"After a few months' acquaintance with
European 'coffee', one's mind weakens, and his
faith with it, and he begins to wonder if the
rich beverage of home, with its clotted layer of
yellow cream on top of it, is not a mere dream,
after all, and a thing which never existed."

Recipe for German coffee

~

"Take a barrel of water and bring it to a boil; rub a chicory berry
against a coffee berry, then convey the former into the water.
Continue the boiling and evaporation until the intensity of the
flavor and aroma of the coffee and chicory has been diminished to
a proper degree; then set aside to cool. Now unharness the remains
of a once cow from the plow, insert them in a hydraulic press, and
when you shall have acquired a teaspoon of that pale-blue juice
which a German superstition regards as milk, modify the malignity
of its strength in a bucket of tepid water and ring up the breakfast.
Mix the beverage in a cold cup, partake with moderation, and keep
a wet rag around your head to guard against over-excitement."
—Mark Twain, *A Tramp Abroad*, Ch. XLIX

The northernmost restaurant in the world

~

King's Bay Service Center
Ny-Ålesund, Svalbard, Spitzbergen
Norway: 78°55′N. Tel: +47 790 27 200

A few kosher restaurants outside Israel

⁓

Kineret Aruba Glatt Kosher Deli
Playa Linda Beach Resort, Aruba, Caribbean

Shanghai Jewish Center Café
1720 Hong Quiao Road, Shanghai

Sylviah Restaurant
1 Regent Road, Cape Town

Dini's Kosher Restaurant
Nuren Jie, Xingba Lu, Jiuba Jie Beijing 100016

Kosher McDonald's
Avenida Corrientes 3247, Buenos Aires

The best restaurants on ships

⁓

Dream Submarine—a submarine in Jeddah, Saudi Arabia.
Speciality: it is half submerged, so that as you eat your fish you can see fish swimming by.
Jumbo Kingdom—a junk in Hong Kong.
Speciality: choose your own live fish.
The Lightship—the world's oldest lightship, London.
Speciality: fish, Danish nouveau cuisine.
New Island—A pleasure steamer in St Petersburg.
Speciality: an ounce of caviar for only 850 roubles—about £16.50.
Odessa—a Russian merchant ship in Amsterdam.
Speciality: disco, bar, hotel and restaurant rolled into one.
And if this doesn't suit you, there are other restaurant ships in the Amsterdam docklands.

The southernmost restaurant in the world

~

Camblor,
Puerto Williams, Tierra del Fuego
Chile: 54°56′S. Tel: +56 61 62 10 33

Stranger, should you come to Japan

~

...then visit the **oldest sushi restaurant**, dating from 1781:
Sushiman, 5-11, Koraibishi 4-chome, Chuo-ku, Osaka
Tel: +81 06 62 31 1520

... and the **best sushi** restaurant:
Kyuubei, 7-6, Ginza 8-chome, Chuo-ku, Tokyo
Tel: +81 03 35 71 6523

And, of course, the **biggest, finest and most amazing fish market**
in the world: Tsukiji. Take the Hibiya subway line to Tsukiji station, but go early, because the market starts at 3 a.m.—and the
cleaning team springs into action by 1 p.m.!

International seafood cooking contests

~

International Boston Seafood Show—14–16 March 2010
Fish-soup Competition in Baja, Hungary—second weekend in July
Ensenada International Seafood Fair, Mexico—second weekend in
September

The most expensive restaurants in the world

According to Forbes, average price of dinner is:

Aragawa, Tokio	$368 (£225)
Alain Ducasse au Plaza Athénée, Paris	$231 (£141)
Gordon Ramsey, London	$183 (£112)
Acquarelle, Munich	$125 (£76)
Alberto Ciarla, Rome	$113 (£69)
Sushi Kaji, Toronto	$109 (£66)
Queue de Cheval Steak House, Montreal	$85 (£52)
El Amparo, Madrid	$70 (£43)
Whampoa Club, Shanghai	$63 (£39)
Boeucc, Milan	$62 (£38)

Restaurants recommended by *Mare* magazine

Futomasa—Speciality: fugu (puffer fish)
Sennichimae 2-7-18, Chuo-Ku, Osaka, Japan. Tel: +81 00 334 129

Botafumeiro—Speciality: precebes—goose barnacles
Gran de Gràci, 81, Barcelona, Spain. Tel: +34 93 2184230

Panama Jack's—Speciality: abalone
Berth 500, Cape Town Harbour, South Africa.
Tel: +27 21 447 39 92

Prir Frakkar—Speciality: whale meat (politically correct type)
Baldursgata 14, 101 Reykjavik, Iceland. Tel: +354 552 39 39

Leo Burdock's—Speciality: fish 'n' chips
2 Werburgh Street, Dublin 8, Ireland. Tel: +353 1454 03 06

Ristorante la Tartana Da Mario—Speciality: mussels
Davette allo scoglio, Via Appia (at 103 kilometres), 04019
Terracian, Italy. Tel: +39 077 370 2461

Natusch—Speciality: salmon in salt crust
Am Fischbahnhof 1, Bremerhaven, Germany. Tel: +49 0471 710 21

Visser Vis—Speciality: matjes herring and prawns
Haven 22, Lauwersoog, Netherlands. Tel: +31 5193 49101

Frontière de Pont Saint-Louis—Speciality: see daily set meal
06500 Menton, France. Tel: +33 49 2418686

Chicama—Speciality: ceviche (marinated raw fish)
35 East 18th Street, New York, USA. Tel: +1 21250 522 33

Munch's Hus—Speciality: stockfish
Bülowstraße 66, Berlin, Germany. Tel: +49 030 2101 40 86

Mercado Restaurant—Speciality: whelks (scungilli) locos
Mexican 617, Punta Arenas, Chile. Tel: +56 612 47 415

Marc-Antoinette—Speciality: parrot fish fritters
St Louis Road, Victoria, Mahe, Seychelles. Tel: +248 266 222

Table of calories

~

Calories and fat content per 100 grams

	kcal	(fat)		kcal	(fat)
Mussels	50	(1)	Salmon (smoked)	163	(7)
Oysters	70	(1)	Herring in		
Flounder	70	(1)	tomato sauce	165	(11)
Squid	70	(1)	Salted herring	175	(14)
Cod	74	(1)	Mackerel	181	(12)
Tench	78	(1)	Herring	195	(15)
Haddock	78	(1)	Pollock	83	(1)
Perch	80	(1)	Salmon	200	(15)
Turbot	80	(3)	Herring (fried)	205	(14)
Pike	81	(1)	Fish fingers	210	(11)
Lobster	82	(2)	Sardines in oil	224	(11)
Zander	85	(1)	Buckling (bloater,		
Plaice	85	(1)	smoked herring)	225	(16)
Sole	85	(2)	Mackerel		
Crayfish	85	(1)	(smoked)	225	(13)
Gudgeon	89	(2)	Tuna	230	(23)
Hake	90	(2.5)	Caviar, Beluga	269	(16)
Prawns	90	(1)	Bismarck herring		
Haddock (smoked)	92	(1)	in mayonnaise	263	(23)
Trout	100	(3)	Eel	280	(24)
Halibut	100	(2)	Squid in		
Pollock (smoked)	100	(1)	breadcrumbs	314	(18)
Rockfish	104	(5)	Eel, smoked	330	(26)
Crab sticks	108	(0.3)	Tuna in oil	347	(31)
Carp	117	(5)	Stockfish		
Dogfish (smoked)	154	(9)	(dried cod)	350	(3)

Sea bream in salt crust

~

About ½ lb. fish per person
  (will be reduced by skinning,
  boning and gutting)
1 sprig of thyme per portion
1 small bunch parsley per person

1 white of egg per fish
3 ½ lbs. of salt per fish
  (preferably coarse sea salt)
pepper
aluminium foil, extra thick

Wash the fish inside and out, and pat it dry. Place the parsley and thyme in the hollow belly, and season with pepper all around. Put the salt in a bowl, then whisk the egg white to a light froth, and mix it with the salt. Add a little water if necessary to bring the mixture to a workable consistency. Put about three feet of aluminium foil on a baking tray and shape it into a fish-shaped container. Spread half the salt mixture over the base of this "dish", place the fish in it, and cover it completely with the rest of the salt mixture. Smooth over the top of the fish with a knife dipped in water. Cook slowly in the middle of the oven for 40-45 minutes at between 350–400°F (175–200°C, gas mark 4-6). Serve the fish in its crust and open it only at the table. People who are fond of salt can eat the coating along with the fish.

From *A Narrative of the Mutiny on Board His Majesty's Ship Bounty* by William Bligh

The allowance I issued to-day, was an ounce and a half of pork, a teaspoonful of rum, half a pint of cocoa-nut milk, and an ounce of bread. The rum, though so small in quantity, was of the greatest service. A fishing-line was generally towing, and we saw great numbers of fish, but could never catch one …

Hitherto I had issued the allowance by guess, but I now got a pair of scales, made with two cocoa-nut shells; and, having accidentally some pistol-balls in the boat, 25 of which weighed one pound, or 16 ounces, I adopted one, as the proportion of weight that each person should receive of bread at the times I served it.

The Chief's head, and an offer you can't refuse

~

"The head of the savage which was last taken off, was thrown towards the fire, and being thrown some distance it rolled a few feet from the men who were employed around it; when it was stolen by one of the savages who carried it behind the tree where I was sitting. He took the head in his lap and after combing away the hair from the top of it with his fingers picked out the pieces of the scull which was broken by the war club and commenced eating the brains. This was too much for me. I moved my position, the thief was discovered and was as soon compelled to give up his booty, it being considered by the others he had got by far too great a share." [The next day …] "I heard the Chief say to the King, 'Had we not better give the white man something to eat?' … [The slave] selected a piece […] I found it to be a part of the foot taken off at the ankle. I made an excuse for not eating it, by saying that it had been kept too long after it was killed. The King replied, it was not half so long as you white men keep your bullum-a-cow! Meaning salt beef, a name derived from bull and cow, by American seamen. Salted meat was considered by them [Fijians] the most unhealthy and loathsome food that could be eaten, and was the means of creating a strong prejudice against the whites for their eating it."

—William Endicott, *Wrecked among Cannibals in the Fijis*. (Endicott sailed as Third Mate with the ship *Glide* out of Salem, Massachusetts, on a trading voyage to the South Seas in 1829.)

The miracle of the loaves and fishes

~

"After these things Jesus went over the sea of Galilee, which is the sea of Tiberias. And a great multitude followed him, because they saw his miracles which he did on them that were diseased. And Jesus went up into a mountain, and there he sat with his disciples. And the passover, a feast of the Jews, was nigh. When Jesus then lifted up his eyes, and saw a great company come unto him, he saith unto Philip, Whence shall we buy bread, that these may eat? And this he said to prove him: for he himself knew what he would do. Philip answered him, Two hundred pennyworth of bread is not sufficient for them, that every one of them may take a little. One of his disciples, Andrew, Simon Peter's brother, saith unto him, There is a lad here, which hath five barley loaves, and two small fishes: but what are they among so many? And Jesus said, Make the men sit down. Now there was much grass in the place. So the men sat down, in number about five thousand. And Jesus took the loaves; and when he had given thanks, he distributed to the disciples, and the disciples to them that were set down; and likewise of the fishes as much as they would. When they were filled, he said unto his disciples, Gather up the fragments that remain, that nothing be lost. Therefore they gathered them together, and filled twelve baskets with the fragments of the five barley loaves, which remained over and above unto them that had eaten."

—*The Bible*: St John's gospel

The miracle fish

The tilapia is a freshwater fish (Oreochromis niloticus) that came originally from the Nile area, and there are early references to it. This is said to be the fish with which Jesus fed the five thousand. The tilapia is often called St Peter's Fish, after the fisherman who became a fisher of men. It has also been dubbed "the miracle fish", "the fish of the millennium" and "the chicken of the ocean". To environmentalists, it is still a miracle fish today, being one of the easiest fish to farm. It is hardy, breeds easily, and is able to grow well in different habitats. It is also popular. The USA is the single largest importer of tilapia, and it is the sixth most preferred species in the country: imports into the USA increased by 61% between 1997 and 2006. It could contribute enormously to easing the world food crisis. The slogan is "eat tilapia instead of meat!" because it can be raised entirely on vegetable matter, and it has the best conversion efficiency of any farmed animal (far superior to cattle), at about 1.6 pounds of feed per pound of meat. This is said to be about as close as we are likely to come to sustainable flesh-eating.

What would Jesus eat?

Americans have been urged to stay healthy and avoid obesity by eating what Jesus ate. Don Colbert, a Florida medic, has published books titled *What Would Jesus Eat? The Ultimate Program for Eating Well, Feeling Great, and Living Longer* and *The What Would Jesus Eat Cookbook*. Jesus's diet as it appears in the New Testament clearly includes loaves and fishes, as at the Sermon on the Mount. In the Last Supper, bread and wine are central. And Luke 24: 42 tells us: "And they gave him [Jesus] a piece of a grilled fish, and of an honeycomb. And he took it, and did eat before them." New Testament scholars confirm that Jesus would have eaten wheaten bread and a good deal of fruit, and would have drunk a lot of water as well as red wine. He would not have eaten meat often, perhaps not more than once a month, or on special occasions. Around Lake Tiberias—the Sea of Galilee—fish would have featured, although for peasants perhaps only in small quantities to provide a relish for their bread. He would not have eaten pigs or prawns, or fish without scales, such as prawns and crabs. Dr Colbert comments that this seafood is higher in arachidonic acid, which is an inflammatory fatty acid, as well as saturated fat that predisposes us to disease. He advises that it is best to eat these animals, forbidden in the Old Testament, only very rarely and in small quantities.

Dietary laws and fish

Judaism and Islam agree that fish with scales are kosher and halal respectively (halal meaning "permitted"). Most Sunni Muslims consider all fish to be halal, while some Shias consider only prawns and fish with scales to be permitted. Some Sunni, mostly Hanifa (the oldest of the four schools of religious law among the Sunni), are adamant that shellfish—prawns, lobster, crab, clams, etc.—are prohibited.

Ichthys, Greek for fish

Said to serve as an acronym for Jesus, Son of God, Saviour
(Iesous Christos Theou Uios Soter = Jesus Christ
the Son of God, Saviour)

Can a fish become enlightened?

There was once a Chinese pilgrim who was making his way to India to acquire sutras, Buddhist scriptures. He came to a wide river, without a boat or a bridge in sight. Desperate, the pilgrim was standing on the bank when a large fish swam up, offered to help the pilgrim, and carried him safely to the other side. "I sinned in my previous life," said the fish. "Can you ask in your temple whether I can make up for my deed and become a bodhisattva [enlightened one]?"

The pilgrim gave him his word, and continued his journey, which was to last for seventeen years altogether. Having obtained the desired Buddhist texts, he set off on his return journey to China. When he came once more to the wide river, the big fish appeared again, and once again it helped the Buddhist to cross. But the Buddhist had long since forgotten his promise. On learning this, the fish became furious and threw the pilgrim off. A fisherman who happened to be nearby rescued the man. But the sutras were lost in the river.

When the pilgrim arrived home, he was extremely angry. His whole seventeen-year journey had been in vain! To vent his anger, he carved a fish's head out of a piece of wood, and hit it with a hammer. To his amazement, on being struck the fish opened its mouth and uttered one letter of the sutras. From then on the pilgrim hammered on the fish head as often as he could, so that after a few years, letter by letter, he was able to piece together the sutras he thought he had lost.

To this day Buddhists strike a drum that looks like a fish.

Woe, woe to Nineveh!

 ow the word of the LORD came unto Jonah the son of Amittai, saying, Arise, go to Nineveh, that great city, and cry against it; for their wickedness is come up before me. But Jonah rose up to flee unto Tarshish from the presence of the LORD, and went down to Joppa; and he found a ship going to Tarshish: so he paid the fare thereof, and went down into it, to go with them unto Tarshish from the presence of the LORD. But the LORD sent out a great wind into the sea, and there was a mighty tempest in the sea, so that the ship was like to be broken. Then the mariners were afraid, and cried every man unto his god, and cast forth the wares that were in the ship into the sea, to lighten it of them. But Jonah was gone down into the sides of the ship; and he lay, and was fast asleep. So the shipmaster came to him, and said unto him, What meanest thou, O sleeper? Arise, call upon thy God, if so be that God will think upon us, that we perish not.

And they said every one to his fellow, Come, and let us cast lots, that we may know for whose cause this evil is upon us. So they cast lots, and the lot fell upon Jonah. Then said they unto him, Tell us, we pray thee, for whose cause this evil is upon us; What is thine occupation? And whence comest thou? What is thy country? And of what people art thou?

And he said unto them, I am an Hebrew; and I fear the LORD, the God of heaven, which hath made the sea and the dry land.

Then were the men exceedingly afraid, and said unto him. Why hast thou done this? For the men knew that he fled from the presence of the LORD, because he had told them. Then said they unto him, What shall we do unto thee, that the sea may be calm unto us? For the sea wrought, and was tempestuous. And he said unto them, Take me up, and cast me forth into the sea; so shall the sea be calm unto you: for I know that for my sake this great tempest is upon you.

Nevertheless the men rowed hard to bring it to the land; but they could not: for the sea wrought, and was tempestuous against them. Wherefore they cried unto the LORD, and said, We beseech thee, O LORD, we beseech thee, let us not perish for this man's life, and lay not upon us innocent blood: for thou, O LORD, hast done as it pleased thee.

So they took up Jonah, and cast him forth into the sea: and the sea ceased from her raging. Then the men feared the LORD exceedingly, and offered a sacrifice unto the LORD, and made vows.

Now the LORD had prepared a great fish to swallow up Jonah. And Jonah was in the belly of the fish three days and three nights. Then Jonah prayed unto the LORD his God out of the fish's belly, And said, I cried by reason of mine affliction unto the LORD, and he heard me; out of the belly of hell cried I, and thou heardest my voice. For thou hadst cast me into the deep, in the midst of the seas; and the floods compassed me about: all thy billows and thy waves passed over me. Then I said, I am cast out of thy sight; yet I will look again toward thy holy temple. The waters compassed me about, even to the soul: the depth closed me round about, the weeds were wrapped about my head. I went down to the bottoms of the mountains; the earth with her bars was about me for ever: yet hast thou brought up my life from corruption, O LORD my God. When my soul fainted within me I remembered the LORD: and my prayer came in unto thee, into thine holy temple. They that observe lying vanities forsake their own mercy. But I will sacrifice unto thee with the voice of thanksgiving; I will pay that that I have vowed. Salvation is of the LORD. And the LORD spake unto the fish, and it vomited out Jonah upon the dry land.

And the word of the LORD came unto Jonah the second time, saying, Arise, go unto Nineveh, that great city, and preach unto it the preaching that I bid thee.

So Jonah arose, and went unto Nineveh, according to the word of the LORD. Now Nineveh was an exceeding great city of three days' journey. And Jonah began to enter into the city a day's journey, and he cried, and said, Yet forty days, and Nineveh shall be overthrown. So the people of Nineveh believed God, and proclaimed a fast, and put on sackcloth, from the greatest of them even to the least of them. For word came unto the king of Nineveh, and he arose from his throne, and he laid his robe from him, and covered him with sackcloth, and sat in ashes. And he caused it to be proclaimed and published through Nineveh by the decree of the king and his nobles, saying, Let neither man nor beast, herd nor flock, taste any thing: let them not feed, nor drink water: But let man and beast be covered with sackcloth, and cry mightily unto God: yea, let them turn every one from his evil way, and from the violence that is in their hands. Who can tell if God will turn and repent, and turn away from his fierce anger, that we perish not?

And God saw their works, that they turned from their evil way; and God repented of the evil, that he had said that he would do unto them; and he did it not. But it displeased Jonah exceedingly, and he was very angry. And he prayed unto the LORD, and said, I pray thee, O LORD, was not this my saying, when I was yet in my country? Therefore I fled before unto Tarshish: for I knew that thou art a gracious God, and merciful, slow to anger, and of great kindness, and repentest thee of the evil. Therefore now, O LORD, take, I beseech thee, my life from me; for it is better for me to die than to live.

Then said the LORD, Doest thou well to be angry?

So Jonah went out of the city, and sat on the east side of the city, and there made him a booth, and sat under it in the shadow, till he might see what would become of the city. And the LORD God prepared a gourd [trailing plant], and made it to come up [grow] over Jonah, that it might be a shadow over his head, to deliver him from his grief. So Jonah was exceeding glad of the gourd. But God prepared a worm when the morning rose the next day, and it smote the gourd that it withered. And it came to pass, when the sun did arise, that God prepared a vehement east wind; and the sun beat upon the head of Jonah, that he fainted, and wished in himself to die, and said, It is better for me to die than to live. And God said to Jonah, Doest thou well to be angry for the gourd? And he said, I do well to be angry, even unto death. Then said the LORD, Thou hast had pity on the gourd, for the which thou hast not laboured, neither madest it grow; which came up in a night, and perished in a night: And should not I spare Nineveh, that great city, wherein are more than six score thousand persons that cannot discern between their right hand and their left hand; and also much cattle?

—*The Bible*: Book of Jonah

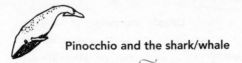

Pinocchio and the shark/whale

"Is this Dog-fish who has swallowed us very big?"
asks the marionette.
"Imagine that his body is one mile long without
counting his tail," his father replies.

In the original Italian story by Carlo Collodi, Pinocchio and his father find themselves in the stomach of a giant shark (pescecane in Italian, i.e. "dogfish") called Monstro, "the Attila of fish and fishermen". In the Disney version (1940), however, they emulate Jonah and end up inside a whale, from which they escape by lighting a fire. The Italian author's real name was Carlo Lorenzini, and he was born and grew up in Florence. The last part of his pen name is taken from his mother's native village of Collodi in Tuscany. In Collodi, which calls itself "the birthplace of Pinocchio", there is a Pinocchio Park with a Great Whale fountain which people can climb into and on to, though they had better watch out for the whale's spout. Disney has obviously displaced Carlo Lorenzini in Pinocchio's "birthplace", Collodi!

How to open a coconut

You will need:

1 coconut • 1 hammer • 1 towel • 1 large nail or a screwdriver

There are two or three black marks on the top of the coconut. Hammer the nail into these indentations, and run the milk off into a glass. Wrap the coconut in the towel and hit it with the hammer until the shell breaks open.

Deadly coconuts

In 2002 two top specialists in the USA, the bat expert Dr Merlin Tuttle and the shark researcher George Burgess, were asked whether it wasn't dangerous to spend so much time around bats and sharks respectively. They replied that these creatures were not at all dangerous compared with coconuts: According to Tuttle, about 150 people die every year from falling coconuts. And large numbers probably go unreported, because in the main areas of coconut cultivation—India, Sri Lanka, and Tonga—no statistics are kept.

It's all a lie!

Coconuts are not nuts at all. They are classed as stone fruit, or (botanically speaking) "drupes", like almonds and walnuts. With a dry husk and a soft middle, this fruit is classified as a simple dry fruit, or fibrous drupe.

9 May 1789

From *A Narrative of the Mutiny on Board His Majesty's Ship Bounty* by William Bligh

In the morning, a quarter of a pint of cocoa-nut milk, and some of the decayed bread, for breakfast; and for dinner, I divided the meat of four cocoa-nuts, with the remainder of the rotten bread, which was only eatable by such distressed people...To-day I gave about half an ounce of pork for dinner, which, though any moderate person would have considered but a mouthful, was divided into three or four.

yeah!

Fish, not flesh

Once it was conveniently ordained that fish was not meat, it became the rule for Catholics to eat fish on Fridays. In Catholic areas, the bulk of all fish sales traditionally took place on that day, and it is said that the Filet-O-Fish sandwich was born in Cincinnati when the owner of a McDonald's franchise there faced bankruptcy because of the regular Friday slump in meat sales among a predominantly Catholic population. It was in 1966 that Pope Paul VI ended meatless Fridays, except during Lent. However, old habits die hard, and Fridays are still important for fish sales. In the USA, nearly a quarter of the population is Roman Catholic, so the demand is considerable, and fish consumption here has increased five-fold in the last hundred years.

Lent is the fish season

~

Traditional Catholics "fast" (i.e do not eat meat) on the 46 days between Ash Wednesday and Easter Saturday. Meat may only be eaten on the six Sundays, which means there are 40 days of fasting.

Traditional Catholics also fast:
- at Advent, apart from Sunday, the Lord's Day—18 days
- every Friday, because Jesus was crucified on a Friday
—43 days
- every Wednesday, because Judas betrayed Jesus
on a Wednesday—43 days.

Russian Orthodox Christians also fast:
- 28 November to 7 January—i.e. before Christmas
- 18 January—the eve of Christ's baptism
- 14 to 20 August—before the Dormition
(passing, ascension) of Mary
- 11 September—beheading of John the Baptist
- September 27 —Exaltation (elevation) of the Cross.

In addition, there are other movable fasting days,
dependent upon the phases of the moon:
- 2 March to 18 April 2009—Great Fast
- 15 June to 11 July 2009—Fast of St Peter

The Coptic Church of Ethiopia has up to 250 fast days.

Friday is still fish day

Strangely, although England has been Protestant for well over 400 years, fish is still typically offered in institutional eating places on Fridays. During the reign of Queen Elizabeth I, laws were passed prohibiting meat-eating on Fridays, although by then the country was Protestant. This had more to do with the preservation of fishmongers, and therefore the fishing fleet, than with religion. The rejection of fish-eating had driven some fishermen into piracy, and others away from the sea, and it was the merchant marine that England relied on to recruit its fighting sailors from in times of crisis. Elizabeth's chief adviser, William Cecil, Lord Burleigh, was responsible for imposing the "no-meat" rule (which was later extended to other days of the week), and that is why he is supposedly satirized in the figure of the garrulous old man Polonius in Hamlet, when Hamlet—pretending to be insane—refers to Polonius as a fishmonger.

Invasion of the warm-water aliens

UK waters are seeing more and more warm-water species moving in. A yellow-fin tuna has been landed off Plymouth, Devon; Spanish mackerel and a shoal of giant ocean sunfish have been spotted (only the second sighting of the sunfish ever recorded in British waters), as well as the rare snake pipefish (a kind of sea horse). There have been sightings of swordfish off Northumberland; octopus in Hartlepool marina; and porbeagle shark off Northumberland—all on the north-east coast of England. North-east Scotland is becoming a centre for whale-watching, and west Wales is attracting rare sharks, turtles, dolphins, and masses of jellyfish. The whales and other cetaceans are obviously moving north in the wake of the plankton and fish that they feed on—trigger and puffer fish, rainbow wrasse, sardines, anchovies, barracudas, and sea horses. There is also anecdotal evidence of the appearance of great white sharks and amberjacks, tritons (large gastropods rarely seen even in the Mediterranean) and baby slipper lobsters.

David Hydes, marine chemist at the Southampton Oceanography Centre, says that these sightings are entirely expected. "There is more heat going into the marine system, so there is more energy and all the seas are changing [as they warm]. We are seeing a gradual push northwards of the plankton. These changes are here to stay."

Squid galore

An unexpected bonus for the Scottish fishing industry is the mysterious surge in numbers of squid off north-east Scotland. The industry has been struggling ever since severe quotas on conventional fish catches were imposed by the EU in 2003. A box of squid can sell for £11 in the wholesale fish market. Off north-east Scotland more boats are now trawling for squid than for their traditional catches of haddock and cod. Squid sales brought in more than £5 million in 2005. One advantage of squid fishing is that the nets used do not trap other species, which avoids the waste occurring when fish have to be thrown back in to comply with current quota rules. However, little is known about the stock of Scottish squid, Lologo forbesi.

A spokesman for the National Federation of Fishermen's Organizations explained this lack of information: "More people have stood on the moon than on the bottom of the sea."

Squid's "in"

~

What is perhaps most amazing of all is that the British have developed a taste for squid. Sales rose by 49 per cent between 2007 and 2008. Contrast this with what James Hamilton-Paterson reported from the deck of a Scottish trawler in the early 1990s, when the crew disdained their gastropod and other catch. "No amount of insistence will make them taste octopus, crab, squid, gurnard or several other species." Not only did they fetch a low price (£9 for nearly 80 kilos of fish), but they were obviously fit only for foreigners to eat, and so they dumped them. "Eat them? I'll never eat one of those things. They all go to France. Places like that."

Don't know it: don't like it

~

But if the Brits are slowly taking to squid, we are still deeply conservative about our beloved fish and chips: for the most part, only cod or haddock will do. The result is that the tasty fish that teem around the UK's coasts, such as pollack and ling, are exported to other European countries, while cod and haddock are imported. There is a neat balance: 75 per cent of the total seafood catch of British fishermen is exported, while 75 per cent of seafood consumed in Britain is imported.

Lobster, lobster everywhere, and not a thing to eat!

Food conservatism is a constant in history. The Pilgrim Fathers almost starved within sight of the richest fishing grounds ever recorded. They had brought no fishing tackle with them, and would not have known how to use it if they had. And being English, they rejected unfamiliar food. The local natives showed the Pilgrims how to catch cod, sturgeons, and eels, and how to open clams. "Oh dear," said the Pilgrims with horrified faces. They would not eat such things … Apparently in desperation, they were eventually reduced to eating lobster. In 1622 [Massachusetts governor William] Bradford reported with shame [in his chronicles] that conditions were so bad for the settlers that the only "dish they could presente their friends with was a lobster".

—Mark Kurlansky,
Cod: A Biography of the Fish that Changed the World.

Et voilà: bouillabaisse
Serves four

½ lb. prawns
16-18 mussels
½ lb. scallops
3 lbs. mixed white fish
 (snapper, red mullet, or
 angler)
1 fennel bulb (cut into
 thin strips)
1 clove garlic, chopped
1 egg yolk
4 fl. oz. olive oil

grated zest of unwaxed orange
bouquet garni (bunch green
 herbs—dill, tarragon, parsley)
1 shot Pernod
1 red paprika
1 red chilli
1 slice white bread minus crust
1 onion, chopped
1 can tomatoes
2 ½ pints fish stock
bay leaf
5 strands saffron

Devein the prawns; clean the mussels and debeard them; remove all but the central white flesh of the scallops. Cube the fish. Cover and place in refrigerator. Heat up some of the oil at medium temperature in large saucepan. Simmer fennel and onion for five minutes, add tomatoes and cook slowly for three more minutes. Add saffron, bay leaf, bouquet garni and orange zest and allow to bubble for a further ten minutes. Stir in all the seafood plus Pernod and simmer for another four or five minutes. Remove unopened mussels, bouquet garni and bay leaf. Meanwhile, prepare the rouille (Provençal sauce): scoop out the seeds of the paprika and chop into small pieces. Grill both paprika and chilli until outer skin blackens. Allow to cool, peel, then remove seeds from chilli and chop it up small. Dip bread in water to soften it, and then squeeze out moisture. Purée it along with the chilli, paprika, garlic and egg yolk, trickling in the remaining olive oil at the end. Ladle bouillabaisse into soup bowls and serve with parsley and the rouille.

Vintage sardines

～

Sardines freshly caught and immediately placed in the best olive oil are called sardines millésimées, or "limited edition" sardines (the "millésimé" refers to the date, or "vintage"). They are considered a true delicacy, and taste best after eight to ten years—especially if turned over every now and then. After this period they begin to deteriorate.

Some vintage prices per 3.75 oz. tin:
La Ponte de Penmarch: $9.49 (£5.80)
La belle Iloise: $4.27 (£2.60)
Sardines millésimées 2003: $8.54 (£5.22)
La Quibonneraise: $7.75 (£4.73)
Filets Bleu 2005, Les Mouettes d'Arvor: $4.75 (£2.90)

California working ...

～

"Cannery Row in Monterey in California is a poem, a stink, a grating noise, a quality of light, a tone, a habit, a nostalgia, a dream ... In the morning when the sardine fleet has made a catch, the purse-seiners waddle heavily into the bay blowing their whistles ... Then cannery whistles scream and all over the town men and women scramble into their clothes and come running down to the Row to go to work ... They come running to clean and cut and pack and cook and can the fish. The whole street rumbles and groans and screams and rattles while the silver rivers of fish pour in out of the boats and the boats rise higher and higher in the water until they are empty. The canneries rumble and rattle and squeak until the last fish is cleaned and cut and cooked and canned, then the whistles scream again and the dripping, smelly, tired Wops and Chinamen and Polaks, men and women, struggle out and droop their ways up the hill into the town and Cannery Row becomes itself again—quiet and magical."

—John Steinbeck, *Cannery Row*

The biggest fish ever recorded

Giant Mekong catfish (freshwater) …. 9 feet 28 inches…646 pounds
Whale shark …………………………45 feet ………74,953 pounds
Leedsichthys problematicus ………….216 feet ……not known
(largest fish ever known; became extinct 150 million years ago)

The biggest catfish ever caught

Was pulled in by Cody Mullenix of Howe, Texas, on 16 January
2004 at Lake Texoma. It weighed 121.5 pounds.

The most expensive fish

In Tsukiji fish market in Tokyo, on a completely normal market
day in 2005, the bids became astronomical. The price reached
$94,307 (£57,676) at the close—for a single fish, a red tuna
weighing in at 285 kilos (628 pounds).

Some other good prices: Golden Almas caviar, the rarest caviar
in the world, goes for $25,000 (£15,000) a kilo (2.2 pounds).

Arowana ornamental fish fetch: $10,000 (£6,000) apiece.

Greek shark

"You must buy belly of tuna in Torone. Sprinkle cumin on it and not too much salt. Do not use anything else, my dear liegeman, except perhaps for a little olive oil. When it is ready, cut steaks from it. When you brown them in a pan, do not use water or vinegar, just the oil, cumin, and aromatic herbs. Grill them over the ashes, so flames do not flare up, and turn the steaks over enough to prevent burning. Very few know or want this divine dish; many are afraid, because this creature is a man-eater."

This is a recipe from *The Life of Luxury by Archestratus*, reputedly the world's oldest cookbook, written some 400 years BCE. It is a guide to Mediterranean cuisine composed in hexameters, and passed down by Athenaeus.

Incidentally, Torone is a town in northern Greece, and the tuna in question is in fact a blacktip shark.

The global drug scene

Around 1492 Martin Behaim constructed the first globe. He marked on it the following products, traded as drugs, spices and medicines:

Pearls, Rubies, Ambergris, Diamonds, Rhubarb, Sugar, Sandalwood, Mumia (crushed Egyptian mummy)

Musk, Aloe, Ashanti Pepper (piper clusii), Cinnamon, Ebony, Camphor, Cloves, Guinea Pepper, Civet, Nutmeg

(B)eat this!

The top ten eating records held by "The Black Widow"

1. Oysters: 46 dozen (552) in 10 minutes.
2. Hard-boiled eggs:
   a: 65 in 6 minutes 40 seconds.
   b: 52 in 5 minutes.
3. Cheesecake: 11 pounds in 9 minutes.
4. Maine lobsters: 11.4 pounds of lobster meat (44 soft-shell lobsters) in 12 minutes
5. Chicken wings: 5.75 lbs (of meat eaten off the bone) in 10 minutes
6. Baked beans: 8.4 pounds in 2 minutes 47 seconds.
7. Tacos (chicken): 48 in 11 minutes.
8. Cheese quesadillas: 31 ½ (four-inch size) in 5 minutes.
9. 3-oz crab cakes: 46 in 10 minutes.
10. Crawfish jambalaya: 9 pounds in 10 minutes.

"The Black Widow" is the name adopted by Sonya Thomas, born 1967, weight 99 lbs, height 5 feet 4 inches, single and living in Alexandria, Virginia, but born in Korea as Lee Sun-kyung. The International Federation of Competitive Eating ranks her among the world's top competitive eaters. Her secret lies in the ratio of weight to amount consumed. She calls herself "The Black Widow" because most of all she loves to beat men. Her preferred "distance" is ten to twelve minutes. She also holds the world eating record for: fruitcake, Big Daddy burger, hamburgers, meatballs, mince pies (in Somerset), sweet potato casserole, toasted ravioli, and turducken (turkey stuffed with duck stuffed with chicken). Her deadliest rival is Takeru Kobayashi, who, like Sonya Thomas, is incredibly slim, and is world champion in the king of eating disciplines, hot dogs, with 53.75 hot dogs in twelve minutes.

Mutiny over poor provisions

22 June 1611—On his third voyage, looking for the Northwest Passage in 1610, Captain Henry Hudson entered the great north Canadian bay that now bears his name. By November his ship, the *Discovery*, was stuck fast in the ice. When at last it was released some months later, the stock of provisions for their homeward journey was low, and the crew cast the captain, his son, and seven sick shipmates adrift in a small boat in Hudson's Bay. They were never heard of again.

18 April 1797—Bad victualling was one of the causes of the famous Royal Navy mutinies of that year, and it was the rapacity of the naval pursers that was to blame: they were swindling their shipmates out of their rations. Although improvements did not follow immediately, the mutinies seem later to have led to better provisioning in Nelson's navy.

18 February 1946—What began as a revolt over food and conditions among a contingent of Royal Indian Navy sailors from a basic training establishment, HMIS *Akbar*, in a suburb of Bombay, quickly became a nationalist rebellion against British rule, spreading across India and eventually involving 20,000 striking seamen aboard 78 ships and in 20 shore establishments.

Fire down below

~

A traditional sea shanty sung while manning the pumps

Fire in the galley,
fire down below,
It's fetch a bucket of water, boys,
There's fire down below.

Chorus:
Fire! fire! fire down below;
It's fetch a bucket of water, boys,
There's fire down below.

Fire in the forepeak,
fire down below;
It's fetch a bucket of water, boys,
There's fire down below.
(*Chorus*)

Fire in the windlass,
fire in the chain;
It's fetch a bucket of water, boys,
And put it out again.
(*Chorus*)

Fire up aloft
and fire down below;
It's fetch a bucket of water, boys,
There's fire down below.
(*Chorus*)

11 May 1789

From *A Narrative of the Mutiny on Board His Majesty's Ship Bounty* by William Bligh

*T*he weather continued extremely bad, and the wind increased; we spent a very miserable night, without sleep, but such as could be got in the midst of rain … In the morning at day-break I served to every person a tea-spoonful of rum, our limbs being so cramped that we could scarce feel the use of them.

Bolinhos de bacalhau

Portuguese salt codfish balls: makes 9 balls

½ lb. salt cod (bacalhau, from Norway or Newfoundland)
parsley, chopped
½ lb. potatoes nutmeg
½ onion, salt, 2 eggs, pepper

Soak the fish in water for at least 24 hours, and then in milk for 12 hours. Poach the fish in the milk until it loses its transparency, and then simmer for about ten minutes on medium heat. Take the fish out and remove bones and skin. Flake the fish, boil and mash the potatoes, and mix the mash and fish. Dice the onion, chop the parsley and mix them in with the fish and mash. Season with pepper, salt and nutmeg. Gradually fold in the eggs until texture is smooth. With two tablespoons form small portions of the mixture into balls about 1 ½ inches in diameter. In a heavy-bottomed skillet or wok over medium heat, warm oil for frying to 375°F (190°C). Fry the cod balls in the oil until golden, and remove to paper towels to drain excess oil. Serve with cold beer.

A good old feed is a good deed

On the second Friday in February every year businessmen and captains meet in the town hall in Bremen on the North German coast to enjoy the Schaffermahlzeit (literally "dinner for hard workers"). It is a big fixture in the social calendar as well as one of the most ancient charity events: the money raised supports sea captains down on their luck. The menu is lavish and has not changed for centuries:

BREMEN CHICKEN SOUP

STOCKFISH

KALE WITH "PINKEL" (A SAUSAGE MADE OF LARD
AND OAT GRITS) AND CHESTNUTS

ROAST VEAL WITH STEAMED APPLES, PRUNES
AND CELERY SALAD

RIGA FLOUNDER (SMOKED SOLE FROM RIGA) WITH
TONGUE, SAUSAGE, CHEESE AND ANCHOVY

FRUIT BASKET, COFFEE

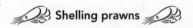 **Shelling prawns**

Prawns still have to be shelled by hand. For that purpose they travel to Tunisia and come back peeled, heading for European supermarket shelves. In the North Friesian fishing ports they are still shelled on the spot, and are correspondingly fresh. But if you want fresh prawns inland, you'll have to shell them yourself.

And this is how you do it: take the prawn between your two thumbs and index fingers, with its back to your thumbs. Break the shell at about the second ring behind the head and pull the tail off. And then the next one. And the next and the next …

A fish meets its end

"… and they affirm that the sea is covered with fish which are caught not merely with nets but with baskets, a stone being attached to make the baskets sink with the water …"

John Cabot came upon the fishing grounds of the Newfoundland Grand Banks in 1497, previously known only to the Basques (long before Columbus). There is a theory that America was discovered as a result of the search for cod. The Spanish and Portuguese knew Newfoundland as "Baccalaos", after the native name for cod. John Cabot's son Sebastian claimed that there were so many fish that his ships could hardly make headway through them. This discovery came just at the right time for English fishermen, whose catches around Iceland were beginning to dwindle.

After five hundred years of overfishing, Canadian cod stocks were practically exhausted. Despite a ban on cod fishing in 1992, we are still waiting for the old teeming abundance to return, although limited catches are now once again permitted. A similar tale could be told of Maine lobster: once so abundant that settlers could pick them up out of the water by the shore, by 1870 they were subject to conservation orders, but the catch dropped from about 24 million pounds a year to less than six million by 1913. However, stocks are now recovering. Japanese pilchards, the largest catch in the world in the 1930s, had been fished almost to extinction by 1994. The Namibian pilchard haul fell from half a million tons in 1965 to zero by 1980.

Save our fish

The harvest of the fishing industry increased by almost forty times in the 20th century: it has been estimated that the three billion tons caught then exceeded the entire catch of all previous centuries combined. But it was not all eaten directly by people. Far more went as fish meal into fertilizer, or to feed animals. Nearly half of the world's seafood is caught in only four areas of the globe: the African Atlantic off Namibia, and a stretch of coast south of the Canary Islands; in the Indian Ocean off Somalia; and in the Pacific off California and Peru. China accounts for half the production of all fish farming in the world.

The United Nations is projecting a forty-million-ton global seafood shortage by 2030 unless something is done. The USA imports roughly eighty-three per cent of its seafood and remains the third largest global consumer of fish and shellfish, behind Japan and China. The American National Oceanic and Atmospheric Administration (NOAA) is working to end overfishing and rebuild wild stocks, but argues that the United States still needs aquaculture to narrow the trade gap and to keep up with consumer demand.

Fishing quotas for North Sea cod

1987 ≈ 197,000 tons
1997 ≈ 130,100 tons
2005 ≈ 31,200 tons
2006 ≈ 23,205 tons
2007 ≈ 19,957 tons

(1 US ton = 0.9 metric tonnes)

Quotas demanded by Greenpeace and the World Wildlife Fund (WWF) for North Sea cod fishing: 0 tons

Daniel Webster's chowder

~

The word comes from the French chaudière, meaning a large iron pot. Traditionally the main ingredients of chowder have always been salt pork, sea biscuit, and either fresh or salt cod—all standard long-life ingredients carried by fishing boats, which still rely on this simple stew as a standby, though the cooking pot is no longer made of iron. The US Statesman Daniel Webster was passionate about chowder, and this is one of the recipes attributed to him:

Party Chowder

"Take a cod of ten pounds, well cleaned, leaving on the skin. Cut into pieces one and a half pounds thick, preserving the head whole. Take one and a half pounds of clear, fat salt pork, cut in thin slices. Do the same with twelve potatoes. Take the largest pot you have, fry out the pork first, then take out the pieces of pork, leaving in the drippings. Add to that three parts of water, a layer of fish, so as to cover the bottom of the pot; next a layer of potatoes, then two tablespoons of salt, one teaspoon of pepper, then the pork, another layer of fish, and the remainder of the potatoes.

"Fill the pot with water to cover the ingredients. Put over a good fire. Let the chowder boil twenty-five minutes. When this is done have a quart of boiling milk ready, and ten hard crackers split and dipped in cold water. Add milk and crackers. Let the whole boil five minutes. The chowder is then ready to be first-rate if you have followed the directions. An onion may be added if you like the flavor.

"This chowder is suitable for a large fishing party."

(*The New England Yankee Cookbook*, edited by Imogene Wolcott, 1939)

Cod clubs

"Wherever there are Norwegian communities, there are cod clubs. There is one in New York and four in the Minneapolis-St. Paul area. The clubs are usually exclusively for men ... Although cod clubs claim to be exclusive and applicants wait years for a place, each club has as many as 200 members. One hundred or more men get together once a month at lunchtime, and the meal is always boiled cod and potatoes with melted butter served with aquavit and flat bread, called kavli. The oldest, most exclusive of the Twin City clubs is the Norwegian Codfish Club at the Interlochen country club in Edina."

—Mark Kurlansky,
Cod: A Biography of the Fish that Changed the World, 1997

Eaten and extinct

Seafarers' diet has at one time included:
Dodo ≈ 1640
Steller's seacow ≈ 1770
Great Auk ≈ 1844
Spectacled cormorant ≈ 1850
Caribbean monkseal ≈ last sighting 1932, believed extinct
(unconfirmed sightings still being reported)

Breakfast with Captain Nemo

Captain Nemo looked at me. I asked him no questions, but he guessed my thoughts, and answered of his own accord the questions which I was burning to address to him.

"The greater part of these dishes are unknown to you," he said to me. "However, you may partake of them without fear. They are wholesome and nourishing. For a long time I have renounced the food of the earth, and I am never ill now. My crew, who are healthy, are fed on the same food."

"So," said I, "all these eatables are the produce of the sea?"

"Yes, Professor, the sea supplies all my wants. Sometimes I cast my nets in tow, and I draw them in ready to break. Sometimes I hunt in the midst of this element, which appears to be inaccessible to man, and quarry the game which dwells in my submarine forests. My flocks, like those of Neptune's old shepherds, graze fearlessly in the immense prairies of the ocean. I have a vast property there, which I cultivate myself, and which is always sown by the hand of the Creator of all things."

"I can understand perfectly, sir, that your nets furnish excellent fish for your table; I can understand also that you hunt aquatic game in your submarine forests; but I cannot understand at all how a particle of meat, no matter how small, can figure in your bill of fare."

"This, which you believe to be meat, Professor, is nothing else than fillet of turtle. Here are also some dolphins' livers, which you take to be ragout of pork. My cook is a clever fellow, who excels in dressing these various products of the ocean. Taste all these dishes. Here is a preserve of sea-cucumber, which a Malay would declare to be unrivalled in the world; here is a cream, of which the milk has been furnished by the cetacea, and the sugar by the great fucus of the North Sea; and, lastly, permit me to offer you some preserve of anemones, which is equal to that of the most delicious fruits."

—Jules Verne, *20,000 Leagues under the Sea*

King of the atoll

here is an island in the South Pacific where the sixty-three inhabitants speak with a strong West Country accent. Now it has been identified as that of Gloucestershire, 12,000 miles away. Palmerston Atoll is the most remote of the Cook Islands, and measures less than one square mile. There is no air transport to Palmerston, and supply ships only call every two or three months. Cargo ships have to anchor outside the dangerous reef, and everything and everybody is landed by island craft.

What accounts for the accent is that all the islanders are descended from William Marsters, an English carpenter and barrel-maker from Gloucestershire, who arrived in 1863 and settled down with his three—eventually four—Polynesian wives. He died in 1899. Not much is known about his early years, though missionaries and yachtsmen did pass on tales of his life on the island. It seems that he ran away to sea to become a whaler at the age of 18, before joining the Californian gold rush in the 1840s, and then taking up trading in the Pacific.

he atoll was uninhabited when Marsters arrived, and he used the remains of shipwrecks to build a church, a school room and housing for his steadily growing clan. He cultivated over 8,000 coconut trees, and exported bêche-de-mer (sea cucumbers) from the Palmerston lagoon to China. It appears he was something of a martinet, and always went armed with a loaded gun and protected by two guard dogs.

As reported by the *Daily Telegraph* in April 2008: "William Wyatt Gill, an English missionary who travelled to the Cook Islands, spoke of him in his book jottings from the Pacific in 1885. He described him as a 'short well set man of 60 years old with an uneasy expression of countenance' who ran the island with an iron fist and had survived at least one attempt on his life." His great-grandson is still ruler of the island, although it is now a New Zealand protectorate. "The reason for the family's survival," says the *Telegraph*, "is put down to its strict adherence to religious laws. It is split into three branches, one for each original wife, and marriage within each branch is strictly forbidden."

Names for sea cucumber

~

Sea-slug * bêche-de-mer * beche-le-mer
* trepang * beach la mar * sea snail * bislama

What has the sea cucumber ever done for us?
PART ONE

~

A delicacy in Japan and China, the sea cucumber became an important trading commodity in the South Seas. Not a vegetable but a mollusc, it was a source of employment for Polynesians, giving them the purchasing power to acquire northern hemisphere products. Whether this was a good thing or not, the Fijians certainly thought so in 1829, when nearly two thousand of them turned out to gather and cure the beche-le-mer that was to be carried aboard two ships from Salem, MA, the *Glide* and the *Quill*:

'When it came to exchanging trading goods for the native labor necessary to obtain the beche-le-mer—the principal article of trade in the islands—a common chisel made by the blacksmith on board from old hoop iron could be bartered for a day's labor. To earn a chisel the islander must leave his hut early in the morning, sail fifteen or twenty miles to the reef and then work knee-deep in the water for six or eight hours gathering the beche-le-mer, a species of sea snail; after which he must carry his spoil to the ship … The beche-le-mer when found on the reef are about eight inches long and three inches thick. They are of a dark brown color, have a rough skin which is thickly covered with slime, and are easily taken. Exposure to the air has little effect on them. After having been purchased by the trading master they are placed in a shallow pool made near the shore where the sea-water flows in at high tide and here the snails are cleaned of slime and then taken to the pot house and boiled about forty minutes. After drying they become hard and are then sent aboard the ship, packed in matting bags and stowed away. When properly cured beche-le-mer will remain in good condition for several years. It requires the Chinese palate to wholly appreciate the peculiar delicacy of its flavor when cooked and served as a table dainty and it was to the Chinese market in Manila that the Glide's cargo was taken and sold."

—from *Wrecked among Cannibals in the Fijis*, by William Endicott, third officer of the ship *Glide* from Salem, Massachusetts, 1829).

What has the sea cucumber ever done for us?
PART TWO

But this was not the limit of its usefulness. The sea cucumber was such a valuable trading commodity that it gave its name to a language, Bislama, an English-based pidgin dialect that is used in Fiji and the Solomon Islands and is an official language in Vanuatu. The name derives from the Portuguese bicho do mar, literally "sea-worm", and developed from the pseudo-French bêche-de-mer or beche-le-mer to an anglicized beach-la-mar, eventually becoming bislama.

What has the sea cucumber ever done for us?
PART THREE

But the sea cucumber was not done yet. In March 2008 came news that it had inspired the creation of a raw material that could one day be used to make brain implants for research on patients with Parkinson's disease. Reporting research being carried out at Case Western Reserve University in Ohio, the US journal *Science* described how the ability of the sea cucumber to tense and become rigid when threatened was helping to create a material that mimics this trick and could be used to make brain electrodes which are stiff when implanted, yet soft and flexible inside the brain. The "architecture" of the new material (it has no name as yet) is based on the skin of the sea cucumber.

What has the sea cucumber ever done for us?
PART FOUR

~

But there's more! It was also thanks to the sea cucumber that early 2008 saw the hope of a breakthrough in preventing malaria. An international team has combined part of the sea cucumber lectin (protein) gene with part of a mosquito gene. The lectin released in the mid-gut of a mosquito is lethal to some of the malaria-carrying parasites that lurk there. This could potentially prevent transmission of malaria by the mosquito to other people. Researchers say that the lectin could be effective against more than one of the four different parasites that can cause malaria in humans. This is important because malaria mosquitoes are showing signs of resistance to current drugs.

~

From *A Narrative of the Mutiny on Board His Majesty's Ship Bounty* by William Bligh

*H*aving again experienced a dreadful night, the day showed to me a poor miserable set of beings full of wants, without any thing to relieve them. Some complained of a great pain in their bowels, and all of having but very little use of their limbs. What sleep we got was scarce refreshing, we being covered with sea and rain ... I served a spoonful of rum at day-dawn, and the usual allowance of bread and water.

Salmon in soy mirin sauce

~

Per person

½ lb. salmon
½ tbsp. brown sugar
1 tbsp. Japanese soy sauce
hot mustard
1 tbsp. mirin (sweet rice wine) or sherry
extra strength aluminium foil

Mix the soy sauce, mirin and sugar in a bowl. Place salmon with skin downwards (if there is still skin on the fish) in the aluminium foil and pour on the sauce. Close the foil around the fish so that it is watertight. Cook in pre-heated oven at 350°F (175°C) for 20 minutes. Take the salmon out of the foil, pour off the sauce into a dish, stir a blob of mustard into it, and serve.

Too much salmon

~

"Salmon is tender and flaky, but hard to digest because of its fat. For a strong stomach it provides a healthy meal, the most nourishing of all fish. Too much salmon often causes stomach cramps, which can only be cured with an emetic. Salmon are often diseased and covered in blisters when they have spawned their eggs. That is how the Irish contracted leprosy, as the Egyptians did in Cairo by eating bad fish from the Nile."

—Eugen von Vaerst, *Gastrosophie* (1851)

It is a fact that salmon are now returning to the Thames in London, from which they disappeared around the 1830s. Well known but possibly apocryphal is the story that salmon were so plentiful in the Thames at one time that there was a clause in the contracts of apprentices stipulating that they could not be forced to eat salmon more than three times a week. Other versions have it that they rioted because their masters gave them salmon as often as three times a week. It is slightly suspicious that the very same tale also crops up in relation to the Rhine in Germany and the Vltava River in Prague (where salmon are now also making a comeback)!

Seaweed wine

~

A wine made from brown laminaria saccharina seaweed is retailing in German stores at £17 a bottle. It is said to taste like a fine sherry and to be extremely wholesome.

Seaweed beers

~

Bière Ambrée aux Algues from Tonnerre de Brest (France)
Kelpie from Heather Ale Company (Scotland)
Galmaarden Tripel Meesters Bier from Huyghe (Belgium)

What seaweed are we having tonight, Mum?

~

Of the world's 40,000 types of seaweed, some 160 are edible.

Arama (Eisenia bicyclis)—Mild, slightly sweet taste. Rich in zinc, fibre, vitamins A and B2. Said to cleanse the blood. Good with salad and blanched vegetables.

Dulse (Palmaria palmata)—Eaten straight from Irish rocks, or with butter in Iceland. Can also be grilled, or baked with a cheese topping.

Hiziki (Hizikia fusiformes)—Black, with a strong flavour. Rich in minerals, but like all algae almost free of fat and carbohydrates. Add to vegetable dishes near the end of the cooking process.

Kombu (Laminaria japonica)—Dark green to brown. Rich in natural glutamines, magnesium, and potassium. Good for broths and soups: remove after a few minutes, and reuse. Goes well with sweeter vegetables such as carrots.

Lato (Caulerpa racemosa)—Small berries that look and taste like caviar. Hard to obtain outside the Philippines.

Laver bread (Porphyra umbilicalis)—This attractive purplish-red seaweed must first be boiled for 5-6 hours. In Wales, it is fried in small cakes with butter, bacon and lemon juice, traditionally not in an iron pan but in an aluminium one. A wooden fork or spoon should be used.

Nori (Porphyra tenera)—This red alga is well known as the wrapping used in sushi and sushi rolls. Toasted, it can be sprinkled on salads, soups or risottos.

Rimarupa (Durvillaea antarctica)—Olive-green, vitamin-rich seaweed, which can be used like agar-agar for thickening. But it has its own distinct flavour and is good with salads and soups. The Maoris used to cut the large leaves up to collect muttonbird eggs in or to wrap fish for cooking.

Rohia (Gigartina)—Reddish, vitamin-rich, to be used as a jelly. Found on many Pacific coasts.

Sea lettuce (Ulva lactuca)—Green, resembling lettuce. Rich in vitamin A, 15% protein. Can be eaten raw or cooked like spinach. Popular in Hawaii and New Zealand.

Wakame (Undoria pinnatafida)—Light green, feathery in appearance. Contains calcium and valuable trace elements. Found in every miso soup, but also in stews, marinades and salads.

Hiziki

~

Per person
1 oz. hiziki (black seaweed)
2 tbsp. mirin (rice vinegar)
1 abura-age (slice of deep-fried tofu)
1 pinch of sugar
½ carrot
3 tbsp. soy sauce
groundnut oil

Soften the hiziki for ten minutes in cold water, and carefully drain off water in a large colander. Julienne the carrot, cut abura-age in strips. Heat the oil in a pan, stir-fry seaweed and carrot for two or three minutes to seal them. Add the abura-age and stir while reducing with the mirin, sugar, water and soy sauce. Serve warm.

Agar-agar

~

The all-rounder among the algae; in fact derived from a number of seaweeds. Substitutes for meat gelatine, thus ideal for vegetarians, as well as for Jews and Muslims, being kosher and halal. More common in Asia than gelatine, it needs no refrigeration, which is not so easily available in Asian countries, and it will not melt down in tropical temperatures. Half a teaspoonful will replace four leaves of gelatine. It has no taste or smell, but contains 80% fibre, and as it absorbs water it triples in size once eaten. This leads to a feeling of fullness, and is behind one of the latest slimming fashions, the kanten (Japanese for agar-agar) diet. It is also used as a laxative. Biologists like to employ it—as "Agar jelly"—in their petri dishes, because they want the bacteria they are cultivating to feed only on the liquid nutrients they are given and not the growth medium: Agar can be boiled to sterilize it at 100°C. Dentists use it as an impression material.

Kobumaki

~

Per person
4 leaves of Kobumaki (kelp)
5 tbsp. soy sauce
6 oz. salmon
3 tbsp. sake
1 oz. kanpyo (pumpkin strips)
4 tbsp. sugar

Soak the kelp for ten minutes (keep the water). Trim the salmon to the size of the kelp leaves, wrap the pieces in the damp leaves, and tie them together with the kanpyo strips. Put the parcels in a saucepan, add the water in which you soaked the kelp, and simmer for an hour on low heat. Then add sugar, soy sauce and sake, and simmer for a further 30 minutes.

Lavender ice with agar-agar

~

2 tbsp. dried lavender flowers
½ oz. agar-agar
3 tbsp. sugar
1 lemon

Bring a pint of water to the boil and let the lavender flowers draw for twenty minutes. Remove the flowers, cool liquid for two minutes. Add juice of lemon and stir in agar-agar until it dissolves. Bring to the boil, add sugar, go on heating for three minutes, stirring occasionally, and pour into glasses. Allow to cool before placing in freezer compartment. Instead of lavender you can use mint or rose petals.

Spirulina

~

Both the Aztecs and the shore-dwellers of Lake Chad ate this slimy stuff. Its correct name is cyanobacteria, and these worm-shaped specimens are sold as nutritional supplements in powder and tablet form, said to be good for depression, high cholesterol, and those who are overweight. They have twenty times as many essential amino acids as soy sauce, 200 times as many as beef; 9% mineral content; a lot of protein; and even more vitamins. And what does spirulina do for the climate? Every kilo of this algae that grows consumes one and a half kilos of carbon dioxide, and produces a kilo of oxygen. Let's have more of it!

This is a blue algae which looks very strange and does not taste good—but is very healthy, and good for the environment.

Samphire

PART ONE

~

Also known as:

sea fennel, sea asparagus, sea pickle, glasswort, salicornia

There are two types of samphire: rock and marsh. Rock samphire is rarer and much sought after, so that lives are risked to gather it, and it is mentioned in Shakespeare's *King Lear*:

> "Half-way down hangs one that
> gathers samphire: dreadful trade!"

It is said that the best marsh samphire is covered by every tide, so that collecting it is a muddy business.

Sea bass and marsh samphire

4 fish fillets (e.g. sea bass)	4 fl. oz. cup dry vermouth
2 shallots, chopped	4 fl. oz. crème fraîche
½ pound of samphire, collected in June	1 tbsp. butter
	salt, pepper, olive oil

Sweat the shallots in the vermouth, add the crème fraîche, and heat up to reduce by half. In another pan, blanch the samphire for three minutes, drain and add to the sauce. Add the butter and purée everything together. Season with salt and pepper. Meanwhile, fry the fish fillets in olive oil. Serve fish plus sauce.

Samphire
PART TWO

~

Marsh samphire does not need fresh water, and has a protein content of 40%. The foodstuff of the future for dry coastal regions!

Further uses:
≈ for fish feed
≈ made into chipboard
≈ as cooking oil
≈ in cosmetics
≈ pressed into briquettes
≈ its ashes are a source
of soda for glassmaking
(hence the name "glasswort')

A few places where samphire is grown

~

Seawaterfarm, Massawa, Eritrea

Saline Seed, Baja California, Mexico

Pukuuo Lagoon, Molokai, Hawaii

Green Garden Samphire, Yancheng, China

Catshark and guitarfish

For five years biologists from the Australian Commonwealth Scientific and Industrial Research Organisation (CSIRO) shopped around in Indonesian fish markets, which led them to discover six new types of shark and ray by 2006:

Roughnose stingray (Pastinachus solocirostrosis)

Hortle's whipray (Himantura hortlei)

Penggali guitarfish (Rhinobatos penggali)

Jimbaran shovel-nosed ray (Rhinobatos jimbaranensis)

Balinese catshark (Atelomycterus baliensis)

Whitefin smoothhound (Mustelus wididoi)

The last journey of the dusky shark

Highly endangered types of shark:

Dusky shark (Carcharinus obscurus) • **Basking shark** (Cetorhinus maximus) • **Great white shark** (Carcharadon carcharis) • **Porbeagle** (Lamna nasus) • **Whale shark** (Rhincodon typus) • **Blacktip shark** (Carcharinus limbatus) • **Sand Tiger shark** (Carcharias Taurus) • **Sandbar shark** (Carcharhinus plumbeus) • **Ganges shark** (Glyphis gangeticus) • **Kitefin shark** (Dalatias licha) • **Bluntnose sixgill shark** (Hexanchus griseus)

Protecting the shark

The National Oceanic and Atmospheric Administration (NOAA) of America joined up in July 2007 with the US Fish and Wildlife Service to expand their ability to analyse shark fins and identify the species from which they have been removed. This move will help to curtail shark finning, which is prohibited in the federal waters of the Atlantic and Pacific, the Gulf of Mexico and the Caribbean. Shark's fin soup sells for £60 or more in Asian restaurants. Sharks are particularly threatened because they are long-lived and slow to reproduce.

The revenge of the shark?

In April 2008 a surfer from San Francisco died after being bitten by a grey shark in western Mexico, the second fatal attack along the southern Pacific coast in four days. Fatal shark attacks in Mexico are rare. No one was previously killed by a shark on the Pacific coast in more than thirty years. Just a few days earlier a man was killed in the ocean near San Diego, the first person to die in a shark attack off southern California in fifty years. On the Atlantic coast attacks are much more common, particularly in Florida, where they run at about twenty-five to thirty a year. But people are a much greater threat to sharks than sharks are to us.

Shark shock

~

Where do basking sharks go in winter? Until very recently, nobody had a clue. These large animals—up to 10 metres long, with mouths a metre wide—move along the western coast of the UK, but disappear in winter, though they were believed to remain on the continental shelf. However, two sharks were tagged off the Isle of Man on the same day, 21 June. One went to the area of the River Clyde in Scotland, which is normal. But the other basking shark, a female, was discovered to have swum 9,000 kilometres to Newfoundland in eighty-two days, three times as far as any other shark on record, and sometimes at record depths of 1,264 metres in water 4,500 metres deep. So it has been established for the first time that the European and the American basking sharks—which move up and down the eastern seaboard of North America—can meet and therefore interbreed. They do in fact belong to one species, but it was never understood until now how this unity was maintained. More research remains to be done: is the long westerly migration sex-specific, as in the case of other sharks? And have basking shark numbers recovered after the ban on fishing them in the UK?

15 May 1789

~

From *A Narrative of the Mutiny on Board His Majesty's Ship Bounty* by William Bligh

The sight of these islands served but to increase the misery of our situation. We were very little better than starving, with plenty in view; yet to attempt procuring any relief was attended with so much danger, that prolonging of life, even in the midst of misery, was thought preferable, while there remained hopes of being able to surmount our hardships.

Legendary oyster-lovers

~

Casanova—*50 oysters before one of his exploits*
Balzac—*100 oysters for lunch*
Bismarck—*150 oysters for dinner*
Louis XIV—*400 oysters before his wedding night*
Emperor Aulus Vitellius—*1,000 oysters at a banquet*

Oyster knives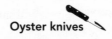

~

Boston stabber—*for big Pacific or American oysters*

Galveston knife—*for Pacific oysters, using the brute force method*

New Haven knife—*good for hinge-opening method with European, Olys and Kumamoto oysters*

Methods of opening oysters

~

Brutal—Get some pliers from your toolbox and break a piece away from the edge of the shell, then slip a thin knife in and cut the adductor muscle that holds the oyster shut.

Classic—this is the method of opening an oyster by way of its hinge. Take the oyster in your gloved hand, with the cupped (more "bellied") side downwards. Chip a little of the shell away at the "beak" or pointed end of the oyster to get at the hinge, which is always set back slightly within the shell. Having reached the hinge, carefully work the tip of the knife through it. Break the hinge and ease the shell open slightly. Then pull the blade gently along the inside of the top shell and separate top from bottom: the top shell should now be discarded. As well as the meat of the oyster there will be seawater in the bottom shell, so hold it as level as possible while pouring off the water carefully. Remove small splinters of shell with the point of the knife.

Oysters in New York

"Impossible to describe how large and small fish teem in the bay: whales, tuna, porpoises, massive shoals of fish. Eagles and other birds of prey circle above the water waiting to pounce on them."
—Jasper Danckaerts, 1680

"The sea around New York produces vast quantities of oysters. You find them above all where the ground is muddy. Less often in sand, and hardly ever among gravel and rocks." —Peter Kalm, 1748

"The lamps burning in the oyster cellars cast a red glow across to the other side of the street. These cellars are the dernier cri; everywhere you see gaggles of half-tipsy young men standing at their entrances. They are on their way to the theatre, the gaming saloon, a bowling bar, the nearest brothel, or perhaps all of the above. A few of them vomit in doorways; too many oysters and bad liquor. In their evil-smelling mouths are mighty cigars of the kind the barkeeper extols as "full flavored."" —George F. Foster, 1850

"The poorer people eat prawns and oysters on the beach. Or sweet things or meat at the tables put out by the hotels. The rich spend vast amounts on something resembling wine, and on remarkable heavy meals which we who are used to more delicate, lighter food would scorn. These people prefer quantity; we prefer quality."
—José Marti, 1881

World oyster-shucking speed contest, 2006

~

*At the Galway International Oyster Festival 30 oysters have to be
opened. Style counts as well as speed—and penalty seconds are
added for cuts and splinters*

Michael Moran (Ireland)	2:21
Hasse Johannsson (Sweden)	2:40
Frederick Lindford (Great Britain)	3:10
Ben May (Australia)	3:13
Heini Petersen (Norway)	3:18
Bernand Gonthier (France)	3:40
Xavier Caille (Belgium)	3:42
Scott Stiles (USA)	3:47
Jason Woodside (Canada)	3:51
Karsten Bonde (Denmark)	3:53
Olli Karvonen (Finland)	4:20
Urs Mueller (Germany)	4:24

Types of oyster

~

Flat oysters (the best)
France: Marennes, Bouzigue, Gravettes d'Arcachon and Belon
oysters (held to be the best in the world) • Holland: Imperial and
Zeeland oysters • Belgium: Ostend oysters • Denmark: Limfjord
oysters • England: Colchesters and Whitstables ("Native
Oysters") • Ireland: Oysters from Galway and Cork

~

Cupped oysters
Germany: Sylt royal • France: Fine de claire •
China, Japan: Pacific rock oyster •
USA: Box oyster, Atlantic oyster, oysters from Blue Point Long
Island, Cape Cod, Chatham and Kent Island

So long, oyster!

~

*T*he European oyster (Ostrea edulis) was long regarded as the queen of the seas. It was a delicacy found growing in abundance from Norway to the Black Sea. But, already completely over-exploited by then, in the 19th century it began to come under pressure from the Portuguese oyster. Two viruses were disastrous for both types. Stocks were devastated by oyster disease in the 1970s. Ostrea edulis disappeared from many of its native habitats, such as the north German coast, but stocks are now being carefully conserved, and European oysters are available, at a price. They are also cultivated in other parts of the world, and healthy specimens—they must have been free of all disease for at least two years—are being reimported into European waters.

Hello, oyster!

~

*I*n the 1960s, farming of the Pacific oyster began in Germany to replace the lost European oyster, which had died out in the North Sea mud flats. As their Pacific charges needed warmer water, the oyster breeders naturally assumed they would stay in their oyster beds.

But in 1998 two Pacific oysters were found in mud flats in Lower Saxony. By 2003 there were already 60,000, and numbers for 2007 are estimated to have been around 2 million. Warmer winters are held responsible. The same change has taken place around UK coasts.

16 May 1789

From *A Narrative of the Mutiny on Board His Majesty's Ship Bounty* by William Bligh

In addition to our miserable allowance of one 25th of a pound of bread, and a quarter of a pint of water, I issued for dinner about an ounce of salt pork to each person. I was often solicited for this pork, but I considered it better to give it in small quantities than to use all at once or twice, which would have been done if I had allowed it.

Oyster steak

1 steak (rib eye), 2 in. thick	1/2 pint beef stock
2 oysters	2 tsps. Worcestershire sauce
2 oz. butter	parsley
lemon juice	oil

With a sharp knife, cut a hollow in the steak. Mix together the parsley, lemon juice and black pepper and fill the hole in the steak with them and the shelled oysters. Seal the hole with a toothpick or thread. Heat the oil in a heavy pan, and fry the steak for two minutes each side. Turn the heat down, cover the pan and keep the steak frying for a further two to six minutes, depending on whether you want it rare, medium or well done. Heat up the beef stock and Worcestershire sauce, stir in the butter over a low heat, and pour the sauce over the steak. Suitable accompaniments are mangetout, Brussels sprouts, sweet corn and red wine.

Whale products

Blubber from sperm whale—oil for clocks and machines,
glycerine, cosmetics, medicines, and lamp oil—until 1860.
Ambergris from the stomach of the sperm whale—for perfume,
to this day (£500 an ounce).
Spermaceti from the head cavities of the sperm whale—for can-
dles and lubrication. For cosmetics—until 1982.
Nowadays jojoba oil takes its place.
Sperm oil—for nitroglycerine and in margarine—until 1960.
Intestines—liver oil, gelatine, hormone pills, fish extract, glue,
tennis racket strings—until 1982.
Whalebone from the right whale—in corsets, for shoehorns,
cigarette holders, and fishing rods—until about 1931.
Foreskin of the whale—as leather—until 1954.

As Henry David Thoreau said
as early as 1865 in his book *Cape Cod*:

"Can he who has discovered only some the values of
whalebone and whale oil be said to have discovered
the true use of the whale?"

"The boats, sufficiently armed and manned, soon got amongst the whales, when the man at the mast-head had orders to inform those on deck of the movements in the boats and to inform those in the boats by signals of the situation of the whales.

"In a few moments we perceived by a great splashing, which one of them made, that the 1st officer had hove his harpoon into one of them. After running under water some time and taking the line out of the boat to a considerable distance, the whale came up on top of the water. The other whales immediately joining the wounded one gave the other boats an opportunity of striking also, which they immediately improved and all three of the boats were each fastened to a whale at the same time. After the whales became exhausted they hauled up to them and lanced until they were dead."

— William Endicott,
Wrecked among Cannibals in the Fijis

Note: Lawrence Waters Jenkins of the Peabody Museum of Salem, who edited Endicott's book for publication in 1923, is sceptical about this as a first-hand report: "This account of whaling may have been abstracted by Mr Endicott from some now unidentified source." It's always best to take seafarers' tales with a pinch of sea salt. Endicott rounds off his book with the words: "I am about to the end of my yarn, yet I might lengthen it by knotting on other strands, but my timepiece reminds me that it is past midnight; so I shall take the liberty to belay this and turn in."

In defence of whaling

"oubtless one leading reason why the world declines honoring us whalemen, is this: they think that, at best, our vocation amounts to a butchering sort of business … But even granting the charge in question to be true; what disordered slippery decks of a whale-ship are comparable to the unspeakable carrion of those battle-fields from which so many soldiers return to drink in all ladies' plaudits? And if the idea of peril so much enhances the popular conceit of the soldier's profession; let me assure ye that many a veteran who has freely marched up to a battery, would quickly recoil at the apparition of the sperm whale's vast tail, fanning into eddies the air over his head. For what are the comprehensible terrors of man compared with the interlinked terrors and wonders of God!…

"How comes it that we whalemen of America now outnumber all the rest of the banded whalemen in the world; sail a navy of upwards of seven hundred vessels; manned by eighteen thousand men; yearly consuming 4,000,000 of dollars; the ships worth, at the time of sailing, $20,000,000; and every year importing into our harbors a well reaped harvest of $7,000,000. How comes all this, if there be not something puissant in whaling?

"But this is not the half; look again … For many years the whale-ship has been the pioneer in ferreting out the remotest and least known parts of the earth. She has explored seas and archipelagos which had no chart, where no Cook or Vancouver had ever sailed … I say that scores of anonymous Captains have sailed out of Nantucket, that were as great, and greater than your Cook and your Krusenstern [the first Russian circumnavigator of the globe] … Often, adventures which Vancouver dedicates three chapters to, these men accounted unworthy of being set down in the ship's common log …

"Until the whale fishery rounded Cape Horn, no commerce but colonial, scarcely any intercourse but colonial, was carried on between Europe and the long line of opulent Spanish provinces on the Pacific coast. It was the whaleman who first broke through the jealous policy of the Spanish crown, touching those colonies; and, if space permitted, it might be distinctly shown how from those whalemen at last eventuated the liberation of Peru, Chili, and Bolivia from the yoke of Old Spain, and the establishment of the eternal democracy in those parts."

—Ishmael in *Moby-Dick*, by Herman Melville

And what it all means

"The sea and the whale represent the primordial unconscious psyche which contains the aboriginal energies of life—numinous, awesome, and terrible. The sea is the collective unconscious and the whales that inhabit it are its major contents, the archetypes ... The whaling industry is thus a paradigm of the heroic effort of human consciousness to confront and transform the raw and aboriginal energies of the psyche."

—Edward F. Edinger, *Melville's* Moby-Dick:
A Jungian Commentary

New England enterprise honoured

~

"Pray sir, what in the world is equal to it? Pass by the other parts, and look at the manner in which the people of New England have of late carried on their fisheries. Whilst we follow them among the tumbling mountains of ice and behold them penetrating into the deepest recesses of Hudson's Bay and Davis Straits, whilst we are looking for them beneath the Arctic Circle, we hear that they have pierced into the opposite region of Polar cold … No sea but what is vexed by their fisheries, no climate that is not witness to their toil. Neither the perseverance of Holland, nor the activity of France nor the dexterous and firm sagacity of English enterprise, ever carried this most perilous mode of hearty industry to the extent to which it has been pushed by this recent people."

—Edmund Burke, British House of Commons, March 1775

Whaling today

~

"Sea Shepherd Conservation Society founder Paul Watson is leading the *Steve Irwin*, which set sail for the Southern Ocean for the second time after dropping in to Melbourne to repair a blown piston. He hopes to have the [Japanese] whalers in his sights within the next week and has pledged to do whatever it takes to stop the slaughter of nearly 1,000 whales—even if it means putting his life on the line. 'We have taken risks for over thirty years so the answer is yes, I am prepared to risk my life in order to save the whales. I have no problem risking one's life to protect an endangered species like a whale. I think that those who dedicate themselves to protecting this planet leave behind the most noble of legacies.'"

—from a report of 7 May 2008, the *Dominion Post*, New Zealand

Bar stools with whale foreskin

On the famous yacht he named *Christina O* after his daughter, the one-time whaling fleet owner Aristotle Onassis had the bar stools covered in leather from whale foreskins. Among those who sat on them were Winston Churchill, John F. Kennedy, King Farouk of Egypt, Marilyn Monroe, Greta Garbo, Grace Kelly, Elizabeth Taylor, Richard Burton, Frank Sinatra, Maria Callas, John D. Rockefeller, John Paul Getty and Eva Peron. Nowadays you can hire the yacht for about £43,000 a day, or £6,000 per person.

Whale-boats

"A whale-boat differs from the ordinary jolly-boat, launch, or yawl-gigs, barges, dinguis, etc. etc., being exclusively for the service of vessels of war—in the following particulars: viz.—It is sharp at both ends, in order that it may "back off", as well as "pull on"; it steers with an oar, instead of with a rudder, in order that the bows may be thrown round to avoid danger when not in motion; it is buoyant, and made to withstand the shock of waves at both ends; and it is light and shallow, though strong, that it may be pulled with facility. When it is remembered that one of these little egg-shells—little as vessels, though of good size as boats—is often dragged through troubled waters at the rate of ten or twelve knots, and frequently at even a swifter movement, one can easily under-stand how much depends on its form, buoyancy and strength. Among seamen, it is commonly thought that a whale-boat is the safest craft of the sort in which men can trust themselves in rough water."

—James Fenimore Cooper, *The Sea Lions; or, The Lost Sealers*

The joys of whaling

⌒

O the whaleman's joys! O I cruise my old cruise again!

I feel the ship's motion under me—I feel the Atlantic breezes
   fanning me,

I hear the cry again sent down from the mast-head—
   There—she blows!

Again I spring up the rigging, to look with the rest—
   We see—we descend, wild with excitement,

I leap in the lower'd boat—We row towards our prey,
   where he lies,

We approach, stealthy and silent—I see the mountainous mass,
   lethargic, basking,

I see the harpooneer standing up—I see the weapon dart from
   his vigorous arm:

O swift, again, now, far out in the ocean, the wounded whale,
   settling, running to windward, tows me;

Again I see him rise to breathe—We row close again,

I see a lance driven through his side, press'd deep, turn'd in the
   wound,

Again we back off—I see him settle again—the life is leaving
   him fast,

As he rises, he spouts blood—I see him swim in circles narrower
   and narrower, swiftly cutting the water—I see him die;

He gives one convulsive leap in the centre of the circle, and then
   falls flat and still in the bloody foam.

—Walt Whitman, *Leaves of Grass*

Not whaling but sealing

"No unnecessary delay was permitted to interfere with the one great purpose of the sealers. The season was so short, and the difficulties and dangers of entering among and of quitting the ice were so very serious, that every soul belonging to the schooner felt the importance of activity and industry. The very day that succeeded the vessel's arrival, not only was great progress made in the preliminary arrangements, but a goodly number of fur-seals, of excellent quality, were actually killed and secured. Two noble sea-elephants [elephant seals] were also lanced, animals that measured near thirty feet in length, each of which yielded a very ample return for the risk and trouble of taking it, in oil. The skins of the fur-seals, however, were [Captain] Roswell's principal object; and glad enough was he to find the creature that pays this tribute to the wants and luxuries of man, in numbers sufficient to promise him a speedy return to the northward."

—James Fenimore Cooper, *The Sea Lions; or, The Lost Sealers*

Long live cod-liver oil

The valuable Omega-3 fatty acids in cod-liver oil with their high vitamin A and D content are good for the heart, skin, and hair. But to avoid overdosing on vitamin D, you should only take cod-liver oil in autumn and winter, because summer sunshine stimulates the body to manufacture sufficient vitamin D for itself.

Whale steak

~

Serves four

4 whale steaks, 1/2 pound each
butter
1 spring onion, parsley
1 pickled gherkin

The whale steaks should be about 1/2 in. thick, and beaten flat by hand. Heat the butter and give the steaks up to five minutes' frying time on each side. Salt and pepper. Serve with parsley, spring onion rings, and the gherkin. Goes well with fried potatoes, salad, and vodka.

The Famous Tay Whale

~

A gripping Victorian tale in "verse" by the famously worst poet in history: William Topaz McGonagall of Dundee

'Twas in the month of December, and in the year 1883,
That a monster whale came to Dundee,
Resolved for a few days to sport and play,
And devour the small fishes in the silvery Tay.

So the monster whale did sport and play
Among the innocent little fishes in the beautiful Tay,
Until he was seen by some men one day,
And they resolved to catch him without delay.

When it came to be known a whale was seen in the Tay,
Some men began to talk and say,
We must try and catch this monster of a whale,
So come on, brave boys, and never say fail.

Then the people together in crowds did run,
Resolved to capture the whale and to have some fun!
So small boats were launched on the silvery Tay,
While the monster of the deep did sport and play.

Oh! it was a most fearful and beautiful sight,
To see it lashing the water with its tail all its might,
And making the water ascend like a shower of hail,
With one lash of its ugly and mighty tail.

Then the water did descend on the men in the boats,
Which wet their trousers and also their coats,
But it only made them the more determined to catch the whale,
But the whale shook at them his tail.

Then the whale began to puff and to blow,
While the men and the boats after him did go,
Armed well with harpoons for the fray,
Which they fired at him without dismay.

And they laughed and grinned just like wild baboons,
While they fired at him their sharp harpoons,
But when struck with the harpoons he dived below,
Which filled his pursuers' hearts with woe.

Because they guessed they had lost a prize,
Which caused the tears to well up in their eyes,
And in that their anticipations were only right,
Because he sped on to Stonehaven with all his might,
And was first seen by the crew of a Gourdon fishing boat,
Which they thought was a big cobble upturned afloat;
But when they drew near they saw it was a whale,
So they resolved to tow it ashore without fail.

So they got a rope from each boat tied around his tail,
And landed their burden at Stonehaven without fail,

And when the people saw it their voices they did raise,
Declaring that the brave fishermen deserved great praise.

And my opinion is that God sent the whale in time of need,
No matter what other people may think or what is their creed,
I know fishermen in general are often very poor
And God in His goodness sent it to drive poverty from their door.

So Mr John Wood has bought it for two hundred and twenty-six pound,
And has brought it to Dundee all safe and all sound,
Which measures forty feet in length from the snout to the tail,
So I advise the people far and near to see it without fail.

Then hurrah! for the mighty monster whale,
Which has got seventeen feet four inches from tip to tip of a tail!
Which can be seen for a sixpence or a shilling,
That is to say, if the people all are willing.

Whale music

Great whales communicate with each other in the deep sound channels of the ocean, where their utterances travel unimpeded across hundreds, even thousands of miles. It was the US Navy that first recorded these sounds, but it was only in 1991, thanks to an initiative pushed through by Al Gore and Ted Kennedy, that the recordings were made available to civilians. For the first time, cetacean experts got their hands on 40 years' worth of data about the movements and vocabulary of whales.

They found that the whale songs, always sung by males, were structured, sometimes lasting for hours, and shaped like musical compositions. They were transmitted to whales in the same area, who sang them too, while different groups in other oceans had their own distinctive repertoire of songs. What is more, the songs evolved slowly. Researchers who came back summer after summer found that the music had undergone subtle changes, which were picked up by all the local whales. This is in great contrast to bird-song, for example, which remains stable over time.

The seas are unfortunately getting much noisier, thanks to motorized shipping and seismic exploration of the ocean floor by oil companies. Apparently there is evidence that whales are trying to sing louder to make themselves heard. Navy use of sonar testing can have a fatal effect on whales. Sadly, whale music may be under threat just as we are beginning to study it. According to an expert, in 2007 the US Navy "suddenly claimed an 'exemption' from the Marine Mammal Protection Act and gave itself permission to conduct whatever tests it wants for the next two years, citing national security as their justification".

—David Rothenberg, *Thousand Mile Song: Whale Music in a Sea of Sound*, 2008

Love guaranteed or your money back?

Traditional but completely useless aphrodisiacs

eel (England) • abalone (Asia) • oyster (Europe) • bluefish (Canada) • fugu (Japan) • shark's fin (China) • lobster (USA) • caviar (Europe) • salmon (Europe) • sea turtle and its eggs (Sri Lanka) • sea cucumber (Tasmania) • sea horse (China) • sea urchin (France) • deep sea angler fish (Chile) • Venus's shell (Japan, Italy)

Questions and answers

~

Q: How many species of sea horses are on the red list of the International Union for Conservation of Nature, listing those species which may not be caught, sold or consumed?

A: All of them. There are up to 50 types: the precise number is not known.

Q: How many sea horses are caught all the same, and consumed or sold as souvenirs?

A: 24 million annually.

Q: What are the uses of sea horses in traditional Chinese medicine?

A: Powdered sea horse supposedly helps against lethargy, nervousness, heart and circulation problems, rashes, and respiratory problems.

Sea creatures that the World Wildlife Fund (WWF) advises should no longer be eaten

~

Alaskan wild salmon from Pacific NW:	Too much by-catch in dragnet fishing for this typical fish-finger fish
North Sea prawns:	First signs of overfishing, and a lot of by-catch
Common mussel:	Too many taken from protected areas, and the natural mussel beds are being destroyed
Sardine:	Overfished in Atlantic and Pacific; unproblematic in the Mediterranean

Sea creatures that the WWF says should not be eaten under any circumstances—they may be the last of their species

~

Atlantic salmon:	Overfished, very rare, a lot of by-catch
Spiny dogfish:	On the red list of endangered species
Norway haddock/ ocean perch:	Overfished, does not reach breeding maturity until eleven years old, so could die out quickly
River eel:	Stocks close to collapsing
Halibut:	Overfished in the North Atlantic. Like all deep-sea fish, slow to reach breeding age, so can die out rapidly. By-catch includes other equally threatened deep-sea species

Cod:	Overfished, a lot of by-catch, perilously low stocks off Newfoundland; threat of extinction in North Sea and Baltic
Haddock:	Stocks still good in North Sea but over-fished in North Atlantic. Much by-catch of threatened species
Plaice:	Overfished. Nets bring in three times as much by-catch as plaice
Sole:	Overfished. Three to six times as much by-catch as sole
Hake:	Overfished, a lot of by-catch
Tuna:	Pacific goldfin tuna stocks still reason-ably good, but bluefins and other tuna species highly endangered; sea turtles and dolphins as by-catch

**Sea creatures that Greenpeace
says it is still all right to eat**

~

Herring
Mackerel
Coley (pollachius virens)
Northern or Maine shrimp (pandalus borealis)
Alaska pollack*
Alaskan wild salmon*
Pacific halibut*

*Only with MSC certification. The Marine Stewardship Council has undertaken to encourage sustainable fisheries throughout the world.

From *A Narrative of the Mutiny on Board His Majesty's Ship Bounty* by William Bligh

*O*ur situation was extremely miserable; always wet, and suffering extreme cold in the night, without the least shelter from the weather. Being constantly obliged to bale, to keep the boat from filling, was, perhaps, not to be reckoned an evil, as it gave us exercise.

The little rum I had was of great service to us; when our nights were particularly distressing, I generally served a tea-spoonful or two to each person: and it was always joyful tidings when they heard of my intentions.

Uskumru dolmasi

Stuffed mackerel Turkish style
Serves six

4-5 lbs. gutted mackerel (a large, fresh fish)	1/2 lb. walnuts
1 oz. coriander seed	1 bunch dill, chopped
6 large onions, chopped	1 bunch parsley, chopped
4 eggs	4 slices white bread
3 tomatoes	3 lemons (unwaxed)
oil	salt & pepper
	1 oz. pine kernels

Cut off the side fins of the mackerel with scissors. Half an inch above the tail fin, break the backbone, and cut through it again just below the head—but without separating the head from the body.

Roll the mackerel across the table with both hands and stroke from top to bottom with your index finger, so that the bone separates from the flesh. Press the bone out of the flesh with your thumb, starting from underneath. Scrape out as much flesh as you can, as carefully as possible—fish skin and head must remain intact. Put the hollowed-out fish in a large vessel, sprinkle it with salt, and cover it with cold water.

Then wash the flesh and dry it in paper. Heat oil in a pan and slowly fry the onions until light brown. Now add the pine kernels and walnuts and continue to cook on low heat for two minutes. Stir in the flesh of the fish, the coriander seed and crumbed white bread, salt and pepper, and fry for five minutes on a low heat, stirring constantly. Take the pan off the hob, and stir in dill and parsley.

Heat the oven to 400°F (200°C). Rinse the fish skin and dry in paper. Put it in a greased, ovenproof tureen, and pack the filling into the fish skin. Garnish with tomato and slices of lemon, and bake for about 25 minutes.

The best sea salt

*According to a blind tasting held by
the gourmet magazine* À la carte

Prices are per kilo (2.2 lbs)
1. La Saunier de Camargue, France. . . £60.40
2. Maldon, England £11.18
3. Halen Môn, Wales. £85.80
4. Danival, Sel Marin, France £1.90
5. Flor de Sal, Spain. £45.43
6. Schenkel, Greece, iodized. £2.84
7. Sale di Mothya, Italy £5.05
8. Sal de Ibiza, Spain. £95.40
9. Rapunzel, Spain, unrefined £2.27

The Ostend Company's profits from the spice trade

Ship's name	Profit or loss in %
Charles Galley, 1715	+ 100
Prins Eugenius, 1718	+ 189
Keyser Carolus VI, 1718	-50
St Joseph, 1719	+ 84
Prins Eugenius, 1719	sunk, total loss
Stahrenberg, 1719	-30
Stadt Weenen, 1720	+ 56
Keyzerine Elisabeth, 1720	-16 (shipwreck)
Carolus Sextus, 1723	+ 104
Concordia, 1727	+ 217

Shell

London, 1851: Marcus Samuel runs an antique business, and begins importing exotic shells to capitalize on the fashion for using them in interior design. He adds other items to his stock—ostrich feathers, pepper, walking sticks—but he doesn't drop the trade name "Shell". His son, Marcus Samuel Junior, has the same passion for shells, and in 1892 it takes him to the Caspian Sea. And while he is wandering along the beach, Marcus has a bright business idea: to export lamp oil from Russia to Asia. Business is good, and soon Marcus is exporting oil to the West as well. He commissions the building of the *Murex* (named after a type of shell, as all Shell ships are to this day), the first tanker to meet the safety requirements of the Suez Canal authorities. In 1907 Samuel's company merges with the Royal Dutch Company to form Royal Dutch Shell, in order to compete with the American giant Standard Oil: it has turned out that there are more uses for oil than lighting and lubricants. A century later Shell is the eighth largest company in the world.

We're all illiterates really

Most trademark logos consist of letters,
but not the most successful:
the Shell logo,
the Nike "swoosh",
the Adidas three stripes, and
the Mercedes star

The Shell logo is the most recognized trademark in the world. But initially the shell used by Shell was a mussel, rather than a scallop. And the scallop was a symbol long before Shell. It was associated with James the Greater, the disciple who was the brother of John the Evangelist. In the Middle Ages James's burial place at Compostela in Spain became a site of pilgrimage third in importance after Jerusalem and Rome, and the pilgrims who made their way there wore a scallop badge to distinguish them; scallop signs along the route told them the direction to take. Apart from its association with St James (St Iago in Spanish), the scallop shell had a practical use, for scooping up drinking water. Its shape also had a symbolic meaning: the ridges along the back meet in a point, just as all the roads taken by the pilgrims meet at one place, St Iago de Compostela. The traditional colour of the pilgrims' scallop is yellow, just like the Shell logo. But there is a story that Shell opened its early petrol stations in California, which had strong links with Spain, and that is why the logo took the Spanish royal colours, yellow and red.

Kahelani

They look like the Shell logo in miniature, they are colourful, they are only found on Kaui (Hawaii)—and they cost up to $600 (£365): they are Sunrise shells (Langford's pecten).

How fish are caught

Dragnets can extend for miles, and are pulled along behind the trawler. Bottom trawling—using dragnets on the ocean floor—wreaks havoc on the seabed because of its rolling effect, while in beam trawling a steel beam holds the net open, and an iron chain ploughs through the top layer of the ocean floor, scaring the fish up towards the net. Both methods result in four times as much by-catch as target haul. Dragnet fishing is less damaging in open water.

In fishing with a circular moored net, or seine net, whole shoals of fish are trapped. The bottom of the net is pulled together, and the fish are caught in something like a giant purse. The trawlers are called purse-seiners, and vary in size from the 20-foot inshore jitney seiners to the giant offshore tuna clippers up to 200 feet long. Nets are now pulled in hydraulically, and are used for fish that aggregate, or form schools, including salmon, herring, tuna, menhaden, sardines, mackerel, and anchovies. By-catch includes marine mammals.

A fine-mesh fixed net is also placed like a wall in the water, to catch passing fish by their fins or gills. There is not much by-catch, but many small cetaceans become trapped.

A drift net is suspended like a wall in the water; a lot of by-catch in the form of marine mammals, turtles, and sharks. Drift nets have now largely been banned.

Trawl lines can be up to 70 miles long and carry as many as 20,000 bait hooks altogether, which can choke seabirds. A trawl-line hook kills an albatross every five minutes.

Fish traps (baskets, creels, pots) are tube-, funnel-, or tunnel-shaped nets anchored to the sea floor. One or more leader nets guide the fish into the entrance to the trap. Ecologically almost harmless, though off-season bans are in place or planned where crustaceans are in danger of being overfished, e.g. the west coast of Scotland.

20 million tons of by-catch every year

This includes 300,000 dolphins and other cetaceans. Year after year, 8,000 porpoises are scooped out of the North Sea alone, and the survival rate for cetaceans once caught and thrown back overboard is not high.

Floating island I

from Jonathan Swift's *Gulliver's Travels*

y Men were sent by an equal Division into both the Pyrate-Ships, and my Sloop new manned. As to my self, it was determined that I should be set a-drift, in a small Canoe, with Paddles and a Sail, and four Days Provisions; which last the Japanese Captain was so kind to double out of his own Stores, and would permit no Man to Search me …

Not to trouble the Reader with a particular Account of my Distresses; let it suffice that on the 5th Day, I arrived at the last Island in my Sight, which lay South-South-East to the former.

This Island was at a greater Distance than I expected, and I did not reach it in less than five Hours. I encompassed it almost round before I could find a convenient Place to land in, which was a small Creek, about three Times the Wideness of my Canoe. I found the Island to be all rocky, only a little intermingled with Tufts of Grass and sweet smelling Herbs. I took out my small Provisions, and after having refreshed myself, I secured the Remainder in a Cave, whereof there were great Numbers. I gathered plenty of Eggs upon the Rocks, and got a Quantity of dry Seaweed and parched Grass, which I designed to kindle the next Day, and roast my Eggs as well as I could. (For I had about me my Flint, Steel, Match, and Burning-glass.) I lay all Night in the Cave where I had lodged my Provisions. My Bed was the same dry Grass and Sea-weed which I intended for Fewel. I slept very little; for the Disquiets of my Mind prevailed over my Wearyness, and kept me awake. I considered how impossible it was to preserve my Life, in so desolate a Place; and how miserable my End must be. Yet I found my self so listless and desponding that I had not the Heart to rise; and before I could get Spirits enough to creep out of my Cave, the Day was far advanced. I walked a while among the Rocks, the Sky was perfectly clear, and the Sun so hot, that I was forced to turn my Face from it: When all of a Sudden it became obscured, as I thought, in a Manner very different from what happens by the Interposition of a Cloud. I turned back, and perceived a vast Opake Body between me and the Sun, moving forwards towards the Island: It seemed to be about two Miles high, and hid the Sun six or seven Minutes, but I did not observe the Air to be much colder, or the Sky more darkned, than if I had stood under the shade of a Mountain. As it approached nearer over the Place where I was, it appeared to be a firm Substance, the Bottom flat, smooth, and shining very bright from the Reflexion of the Sea below. I stood upon a Height about two Hundred Yards from the Shoar, and saw this vast Body descending almost to a Parallel with me, at less than an English Mile Distance. I took out my Pocket-Perspective, and could plainly discover Numbers of People moving up and down the Sides of it, which appeared to be sloping, but what those People were doing, I was not able to distinguish.

The natural Love of Life gave me some inward Motions of Joy; and I was ready to entertain a Hope, that this Adventure might some Way or other help to deliver me from the desolate Place and Condition I was in. But, at the same Time, the Reader can hardly conceive my Astonishment, to behold an Island in the Air, inhabited by Men, who were able (as it should seem) to raise or sink, or put it into a progressive Motion, as they pleased. But not being, at that Time, in a Disposition to philosophise upon this Phaenomenon, I rather chose to observe what Course the Island would take; because it seemed for a while to stand still. Yet, soon after it advanced nearer; and I could see the Sides of it, encompassed with several Gradations of Galleries and Stairs, at certain Intervals, to descend from one to the other. In the lowest Gallery, I beheld some People fishing with long Angling Rods, and others looking on. I waved my Cap, (for my Hat was long since worn out,) and my Handkerchief towards the Island; and upon its nearer approach, I called and shouted with the utmost Strength of my Voice; and then looking circumspectly, I beheld a Crowd gather to that Side which was most in my View. I found by their pointing towards me and to each other, that they plainly discovered me, although they made no Return to my Shouting. But I could see four or five Men running in great Haste up the Stairs to the top of the Island, who then disappeared. I happened rightly to conjecture, that these were sent for Orders to some Person in Authority upon this Occasion.

The Number of People increased; and in less than half an Hour the Island was moved and raised in such a Manner, that the lowest Gallery appeared in a Parallel of less than an Hundred Yards Distance from the Height where I stood. I then put my self into the most suppli-cating Postures, and spoke in the humblest Accent, but received no Answer. Those who stood nearest over against me, seemed to be Persons of Distinction, as I supposed by their Habit. They conferred earnestly with each other, looking often upon me. At length one of them called out in a clear, polite, smooth Dialect, not unlike in Sound to the Italian; and therefore I returned an Answer in that Language, hoping at least that the Cadence might be more agreeable to his Ears. Although neither of us under-stood the other, yet my Meaning was easily known, for the People saw the Distress I was in.

They made Signs for me to come down from the Rock, and go towards the Shoar, which I accordingly did; and the flying Island being raised to a convenient Height, the Verge directly over me, a Chain was let down from the lowest Gallery, with a Seat fastned to the Bottom, to which I fixed my self, and was drawn up by Pullies.

Floating island II

~

from Yann Martel's *The Life of Pi*

he island had no soil. Not that the trees stood in water. Rather, they stood in what appeared to be a dense mass of vegetation, as sparkling green as the leaves. Who had ever heard of land with no soil? With trees growing out of pure vegetation?…I looked about to see if there were sharks. There were none. I turned on my stomach, and holding on to the tarpaulin, I slowly brought a leg down. My foot entered the sea. It was pleasingly cool. The island lay just a little further down, shimmering in the water … The combined shock of solid land and cool water gave me the strength to pull myself forward onto the island … What was this strange, tubular seaweed, so intricately entangled? Was it edible? … I bit into it. My chops were in for a shock. The inner tube was bitterly salty—but the outer was not only edible, it was delicious … sweet … I ate till there was a regular moat around me. A solitary tree stood about two hundred feet away. It was the only tree downhill from the ridge, which seemed a very long way off. I say ridge; the word perhaps gives an incorrect impression of how steep the rise from the shore was. The island was low-lying, as I've said … The tree did indeed grow right out of the algae … There was not the least trace of soil … The island was carnivorous … The island attracted saltwater fish into its subterranean tunnels—how, I don't know; perhaps fish ate the algae as gluttonously as I did. They became trapped … At night the predatory algae turned highly acidic and the ponds became vats of acid that digested the fish.

Floating island III

~

from Homer's *The Odyssey, Book X*,
from the famous 17th-century translation
by George Chapman

To the Æolian island we attain'd,
That swum about still on the sea, where reign'd
The God-lov'd Æolus Hippotades.
A wall of steel it had; and in the seas
A wave-beat-smooth rock moved about the wall.
Twelve children in his house imperial
Were born to him; of which six daughters were,
And six were sons, that youth's sweet flower did bear.
His daughters to his sons he gave as wives;
Who spent in feastful comforts all their lives,
Close seated by their sire and his grave spouse.
Past number were the dishes that the house
Made ever savour; and still full the hall
As long as day shined; in the night-time, all
Slept with their chaste wives, each his fair carved bed
Most richly furnish'd; and this life they led.

Floating island III continued

~

from Homer's *The Odyssey*,
translation by Samuel Butler, 1900

T hence we went on to the Aeoli island where lives Aeolus
son of Hippotas, dear to the immortal gods. It is an
island that floats (as it were) upon the sea, iron bound
with a wall that girds it. Now, Aeolus has six daughters and six lusty
sons, so he made the sons marry the daughters, and they all live
with their dear father and mother, feasting and enjoying every con-
ceivable kind of luxury. All day long the atmosphere of the house
is loaded with the savour of roasting meats till it groans again, yard
and all; but by night they sleep on their well-made bedsteads, each
with his own wife between the blankets. These were the people
among whom we had now come.

18 May 1789

~

From *A Narrative of the Mutiny on Board His Majesty's
Ship Bounty* by William Bligh

I n the morning the rain abated, when we stripped, and
wrung our cloaths through the sea-water, as usual, which
refreshed us wonderfully. Every person complained of violent
pain in their bones: I was only surprised that no one was yet
laid up. Served one 25th of a pound of bread, and a quarter of
a pint of water, at supper, breakfast, and dinner, as customary.

Floating island IV

◡

from a press release from the Swiss Center for Electronics
and Microtechnology (CSEM) in Neuchâtel, October 2007

ast May, CSEM presented its concept of floating "Solar
Islands" in the presence of Sheikh Saud Bin Saqr Al
Qasimi, Crown Heir to the Ras Al-Khaimah Emirate (one
of the seven states of the United Arab Emirates), and at the same
time announced its plans to build the first prototype of a solar
island in the region.

Construction is now going ahead, at a cost of $5 million (£3
million). The solar island will be 0.62 miles in diameter, will float
on a ring-shaped raft about two miles offshore, and will generate
1 megawatt of energy by heating water to produce vapour. The
scheme relies on at least 350 days of sunshine per year—available
in the UAE. Questions remain about how the island will cope with
bad weather. And environmentalists are concerned about the
island's impact on the marine environment.

Herring pasties

◡

Serves four

1/2 lb. herring soaked in milk	2 oz. sour cream
1/2 lb. white flour	1 onion, chopped
1/2 lb. butter	1 teaspoon sugar
6 oz. potatoes, boiled	pepper
2 egg yolks	salt

Knead together the flour, half of the butter, one egg yolk and 1 oz.
sour cream. Store the dough for about two hours in the refrigerator. Then roll it out thin, cut into hand-sized squares, and make into

pouches. Purée the herring, onion and potatoes, stir in the rest of the sour cream, one egg yolk, sugar, the other half of the butter, and pepper, then fill the dough pouches with the mixture. Brush them with egg yolk and bake at 400°F (200°C, gas mark 6). Very British.

Farting herrings

Pacific and Atlantic herrings (Clupea pallasii and Clupea harengus) make noises. Microbiologists Ben Wilson, Robert S. Batty and Lawrence M. Dill established that the signals, mostly emitted at night, had a frequency of 1.7 to 22 kHz, and lasted between 0.6 and 7.6 seconds. The fish were monitored while swimming around in a 110-gallon tank. The amplitude could not be measured precisely, but the three scientists estimate a sound pressure of 143dB re IPa to 5'10". It appears that these nocturnal noises, emanating from the region of the anus, are used for communication and to guide other fish in the right direction. Quite rightly, Ben Wilson, Robert S. Batty and Lawrence M. Dill were awarded the 2004 Nobel prize for biology. We congratulate them retrospectively.

In the same year Jillian Clarke, a high school intern at the University of Illinois, won the IgNobel prize for health policy. She was investigating the so-called 5 Second Rule, which most Americans appear to believe in, and which holds that any food dropped on the floor will be safe from germs if picked up before a count of five. She found that the floor at the University of Illinois was not dirty enough to produce any significant contamination of the sample food—slices of bread and bologna sausage. Dirtier surfaces had to be tried. However, a very small number of bacteria can cause illness. It appears that germs can pounce on food within two seconds of its hitting the floor, and they then multiply rapidly, so that it is hardly safe to leave your sandwich on the ground for as long as five seconds before picking it up. It is said that the 5 Second Rule originated with Genghis Khan, though he had a more relaxed attitude to the time question, declaring that any food that had fallen on the floor after a banquet would be safe to eat ("Trust me, the Great Khan") for up to twelve hours.

Slang terms for herring

Herring used to be so common (in both senses) that people seemed to feel the need to dress it up as something else:

Two-Eyed Steak:

> Yarmouth bloater, a salted, lightly smoked herring: after the town in Norfolk

Yarmouth Capon:

> herring: see above

Glasgow Magistrate:

> superior herring: after the Scottish city

Atlantic Ranger; also "sea-rover": herring

Billingsgate Pheasant:

> red herring: after the famous London fish market

Digby Chicken or Digby Duck:

> herring/smoked herring: after Digby, Nova Scotia

Dunbar Wether:

> red herring: after the town in Scotland

Gourock Ham:

> salted herring: after Gourock on the Clyde, a noted Scottish fishing village until the 1870s

Taunton Turkey:

> herring: after the town in Devon

Floating island V

ruce Kania of Montana has invented a floating island designed to mimic nature and act as a kind of filter to reduce excess nutrients in any body of water, including the oceans. The islands are usually anchored, but can also be free-floating, and could even provide new land mass for human habitation. Inspired by the floating peat bogs of northern Wisconsin, they are based on a kind of wadding, made from recycled plastic drinking bottles, formed into layers which are buoyant and can be shaped as required. Plants are inserted into pockets, and their roots penetrate the layers to reach the water. Microbes clinging to the island as the plants grow remove the surplus nutrients from the water, and the plants convert them into further growth. Extracting the excess nutrients hinders the growth of damaging algae. The islands are also man-made miniature wetlands, offering a haven to fish and birds. Even a "dead zone" such as the mouth of the Mississippi where it deposits industrial and agricultural effluent in the Gulf of Mexico could be brought back to life by the action of artificial islands as giant filters. Based in Shepherd, Montana, Bruce Kania's firm BioHaven Floating Islands has been selling his invention worldwide since July 2005. See www. floatingislandinternational.com

Floating island VI

~

ne day in January 1988 two companions and I were in a
skiff midway between two islands in the South China Sea
when we spotted something curious in the water ahead.
There was a ragged patch like floating seaweed or the top of a reef
as the tide begins to fall. We knew the area well; we were far out in
a deep channel where there were no reefs. Also puzzling were the
antics of a small white tern which was standing, fluttering and fluttering its wings as if in some difficult feat of balancing on this
patch. As we neared we could smell it before we finally identified
it as a mass of rotting animals. We identified fish, a baby dolphin
and various bird carcasses. The tern's desperate agitations increased
with our approach and we could now see that its feet were caught
in the nearly invisible meshes of a ghost net, a fragment of drift net
which floats and continues to catch almost any animal that comes
into contact with it. With some difficulty we freed the little tern, the
bottom of the skiff whispering over nylon and fins and bumping
softly among the heavier corpses. There was nothing else to be
done. Sooner or later, the gases of putrefaction having been
released, the mass would sink beneath its own weight until fresh
gas was generated or its heavier contents broke up sufficiently to
filter out between the meshes. Then it would rise to the surface
once more.

James Hamilton-Paterson,
Seven-Tenths: The Sea and its Thresholds

How turtles navigate, and why it matters

These tiny defenceless sea turtles embark on this 8,000-mile migration around the Atlantic, and they do it alone without following other turtles, says Dr Kenneth Lohmann, professor of biology in the University of North Carolina at Chapel Hill. Two inches long when it emerges from its eggshell on the eastern Florida coast, the Atlantic loggerhead turtle heads straight down the beach for the Gulf Stream, later finding the North Atlantic gyre, a current that whirls clockwise around the Sargasso Sea. Moving east across the Atlantic, it rounds the Azores, paddling south past the Canary and Cape Verde Islands, and finally back to its natal home on a North American shore. All the while its instincts keep it within a warm, nutritious current, and away from colder waters. Professor Lohmann has found out how it does it: the answer lies in the variations in the earth's magnetic field.

He experimented with baby turtles in a tank surrounded by a huge electric coil, to simulate the magnetic fields at three different locations.

When the tiny turtles were exposed to a magnetic field mimicking one off Portugal, for example, they correctly turned south as they would at that location to stay with the warm current. Nobody has ever found out how "natal homing" works—how turtles manage to find their way back to their own breeding beach to lay their eggs. But Professor Lohmann thinks we now have the answer: they navigate by magnetic fields, enabling them to find a precise "magnetic address".

This research has enormous implications for conservation work. Whereas most conservation efforts are now directed at whole species, it cannot be assumed that any gap in local stock can be filled by importing turtles from another part of the world, as they would be imprinted with a different magnetic field map. We need to conserve specific populations. It is possible that fish carry a similar magnetic map, and according to Professor Lohmann this could explain why low fish populations in one region do not benefit from a spillover of the same species from another location.

Save our turtles!

All sea turtles are listed as threatened or endangered under the US Endangered Species Act. The prime sea-turtle nesting areas are on the Gulf Coast of Alabama, where females return to lay their eggs on the same white-sand beaches where they were born decades before.

The loss of critical sea-turtle habitat across the world has made the survival of every individual sea turtle a priority. In America, an organization called Share the Beach Sea Turtle Volunteers has been formed to assist sea turtles in their battle against extinction. They patrol the beaches, guiding tiny turtles that head the wrong way carefully back towards the water.

The educated Mock Turtle

"Once," said the Mock Turtle at last, with a deep sigh,
"I was a real Turtle …"
"When we were little," the Mock Turtle went on at last,
"we went to school in the sea …
I only took the regular course."
"What was that?" inquired Alice.
"Reeling and Writhing, of course, to begin with,"
the Mock Turtle replied;
"and then the different branches of Arithmetic:
Ambition, Distraction, Uglification, and Derision."

from *Alice's Adventures in Wonderland*, by Lewis Carroll

Mock turtle soup

Serves four to six

2 lbs. oxtail (or beef or pork goulash, or chicken,
   or tripe, or calf's foot, or calf's head)
3 tbsp. flour (for the traditional version)
4 fl. oz. olive oil (half can be replaced by butter)
4 or 5 spring onions, chopped
1 pint fish stock or chicken stock
1 onion, chopped
2 hard-boiled eggs
6 oz. peeled tomatoes
4 button mushrooms
small bunch parsley, chopped
1 stick celery, chopped
a touch of sherry

Cut the meat up small, fry over quickly, and set aside. Brown the onions in a large saucepan, add flour and sweat slowly, adding in succession tomatoes, celery, parsley, spring onions, mushrooms, and stock. Put the meat in the saucepan and cook until very tender—this may take up to two and a half hours! Then season to taste (pepper, sherry).

This 19th-century dish was a substitute for real, and expensive, turtle soup. Calf's head and offal were served instead of green turtle. Nowadays the preferred option is oxtail. As with all soups, everyone swears by their own ingredients. We swear by the above.

The turtle in myth and fantasy

It is a turtle that underlies both the world and the success of Terry Pratchett, the best-selling children's novelist (sales second only to J. K. Rowling's). In his *Discworld* fantasy he falls back on Hindu mythology and rests the world on the back of a gigantic turtle called Great A'Tuin, on which stand four elephants bearing the world-disc. In Pratchett's own words:

> "The world rides through space on the back of a turtle. This is one of the great ancient world myths, found wherever men and turtles are gathered together; the four elephants were an Indo-European sophistication. The idea has been lying in the lumber room of legend for centuries. All I had to do was grab it and run away before the alarms went off."

Endearingly, the Giant Star Turtle occasionally rolls over onto its back to avoid threatening objects in space, just as real turtles turn belly-up with their flippers in the air as protection from sharks.

Aquatic nuisance species (1)

Ninja turtles

With the Teenage Mutant Ninja Turtles fad of the 1970s and 80s, there was a spike in the sale of red-eared terrapins, *Trachemys scripta elegans*. After the craze for keeping the red-eared sliders (as they are also known) had passed, people disposed of them in the wild, including areas where they do not occur naturally, risking upsetting the ecology of that area. Abandoned red-eared sliders can now be found all over most of North America and many other countries. They have a vicious bite that can cause serious injury. In Britain they have ravaged native flora and fauna, including fish, toads, and newts, as well as savaging ducklings in ornamental ponds. In 1997, the importation of terrapins into the UK for any-thing other than scientific purposes was banned. By 2002, there were so many unwanted terrapins in the country that a charity was set up with the help of entrepreneur Richard Branson and his Virgin Express company to round them up and send them to Italy, where there is a terrapin centre. It is run by an Italian charity, Carapax, in Tuscany, where the warm climate and habitat resem-ble the bayou and swamps of the turtles' American homeland. In April 2007, conservation rangers on London's Hampstead Heath were still rounding up 150 feral red-eared terrapins, which were terrorizing local wildlife and invading bathing ponds.

In the USA, by the mid-1970s half a million children and infants were diagnosed as having turtle-related salmonella, and as early as 1975 the Food and Drug Administration prohibited the purchase of any turtles under 4 inches in length. But according to American Tortoise Rescue of LA and the New York Turtle and Tortoise Society, throughout the country in 2007 tiny turtles were still being sold by vendors on street corners and in shopping malls, in front of museums, and even in pet stores, for $2 to $10 (£1 to £6). Imported from Mexico and harvested from Louisiana, they have a 25-year lifespan and are often infected with salmonella.

Maggots for the orfe

Which bait for which fish?

Earthworm — eel, perch, bream, roach, carp, eel-pout, pike
Muckworm — tench, orfe, crucian carp
Muckworm in batches — eel, eel-pout, perch
Mealworm — roach, bream, rudd
Maggot — orfe, bream, perch, nase, rudd, roach, tench
Midge/mosquito larva — roach
Angleworm — eel, chub, grayling, brook trout, red-bellied or Dolly
    Varden trout, barbel, perch, bream, tench, carp, nase, ide, rain-
    bow trout, roach, rudd, eel-put, asp, Wels catfish
Dough (pasta, bread) — chub, barbel, carp, nase, ide, rainbow trout,
    roach, rudd, tench
Dead fish as bait — eel, chub, brook trout, red-bellied/Dolly Varden
    trout, perch, pike, Danube salmon/huchen, asp, rainbow trout,
    eel-pout, lake trout, lake char, Wels catfish, pike
And for your gourmet victims:
    Fish scraps — for eel, perch, and eel-pout
    Cheese — for barbel, chub, and tench
    Maize and potato — for carp
    Prawns — for salmon

Anglers' argot

Blinker   — the traditional bait, a metallic oval, often dented and embel-
                lished with pearls and feathers.
Jerk bait — deceptively real-looking imitation fish, which the angler jerks.
Wobbler — fish made from wood or synthetic materials with a triple-
                pointed hook on the belly and the tail fin respectively.
Spinner   — rotating metallic form with triple-pointed hook.

Aquatic nuisance species (2)

Zebra mussels

The 100th Meridian Initiative is a cooperative effort to stop the westward spread of zebra mussels and other aquatic nuisance species in North America. These small freshwater molluscs (Dreissena polymorpha), the size of a thumbnail, come in ships' water ballast from Eastern Europe, and have been steadily invading America's and the UK's rivers and lakes. They upset ecosystems, threaten native wildlife, and damage structures. Millions of pounds are spent each year trying to control these small pests, but there is no easy solution. They spell trouble for native mussels and clams; they can colonize a clam shell so that it cannot open its shell to eat. Some native mussels have been found with more than 10,000 zebra mussels attached to them. It is true that they also provide fodder for native birds, fish and other animals. Migratory ducks have been known to change their flight patterns in response to zebra mussel colonies. But these native species do not feed heavily enough on zebra mussels to keep the populations under control.

They present problems for:

Navigation, boating and industry: they cluster in water intake pipes and power plants, and clog up boat hulls and the underwater parts of outboard motors, as well as insinuating themselves into engine cooling systems.

Navigational buoys, docks, and other structures in the water: buoys have been known to sink out of sight under their weight.

Beaches: they foul the shoreline, cutting bathers' feet with their sharp shells.

They are so tough and resistant that nothing seems to destroy them!

The Great Lakes: some facts

- The Laurentian Great Lakes of North America—Ontario, Erie, Huron, Michigan and Superior—hold more than 6,000 trillion gallons of water.
- If the volume of Great Lakes water were spread over a surface area the size of the lower 48 states, it would create a lake nearly ten feet deep.
- With its 3,288 miles of Great Lakes shoreline, Michigan has a longer coastline than any other state except Alaska.
- The five Great Lakes hold one-fifth of the world's surface fresh water.
- The lakes sustain the livelihoods of ten per cent of the US population, according to the US Fish and Wildlife Service.
- They supply water to one-third of all Canadians and one-seventh of all Americans.
- Since 1800, more than 160 exotic aquatic organisms (including plants, fish, algae and mollusks) have become established in the Great Lakes.
- More than one-third of exotic species in the lakes have been introduced in the last forty years.
- In 1986, twenty species of native mussels lived in Lake St Clair, part of the waterway between Lake Huron and Lake Erie. Two years later, zebra mussels invaded the lake. By 1997, none of the native mussels were left except in a few shallower places.
- A new invader is identified in the Lakes about every seven months, faster than scientists can study them.

The Great Lakes: dead or alive?

In 1969 a floating oil slick burned for hours on the Cuyahoga River in Cleveland, Ohio, where the waterway empties into Lake Erie. This was the defining moment that triggered newspaper headlines like "Lake Erie is dead". It was an urban myth throughout the 1960s that Lake Erie was biologically extinct and could never be revived. In fact, both sport and commercial fishing continued uninterrupted up to the present day.

But it is true that all of the Great Lakes were in trouble, none more so than Lake Erie. The problem was caused by increasing levels of the nutrient phosphorus in the water and in bottom sediments. Algal blooms were produced by high nitrogen levels; the decomposition of algae led to extensive seasonal anoxic (oxygen-starved) areas or dead zones in the lake, which were expanding rapidly in the 1970s. The rotting algal masses and dead fish littering the shoreline created the widespread impression of Lake Erie as a dead lake.

The revival of the lakes, and new threats

A US-Canadian agreement in 1972 reduced dumping and run-off of phosphorus in the lakes, and Congress passed the Clean Water Act. Although a dead zone persists in the central Lake Erie basin in late summer, the US Environmental Protection Agency is on the case. The "Healing Our Waters—Great Lakes Coalition" is a watchdog group that consists of more than 100 zoos, aquariums, museums, and hunting, fishing and environmental organizations representing millions of people committed to restoring and protecting the Great Lakes. The Michigan Senate has had a bipartisan Great Lakes Conservation Task force in place since 2002. Research shows that Erie, although under stress like all the Great Lakes, is today the most biologically diverse and vibrant of all. Fish stocks have declined, but perch, walleye, and smallmouth bass, for example, are making a comeback. There have been enormous improvements in the last three decades, but threats remain:

- Toxic contamination continues, though toxins like lead have declined, and phosphates have been much reduced.

- There is still nonpoint source pollution and excessive nutrient run-off; nitrates are still a concern.

- There is the invasion of exotic species, especially eel lampreys (since the 1950s), and zebra and quagga mussels. The opening of the St Lawrence Seaway in 1959 brought transoceanic shipping into the lakes, and sped up the introduction of exotic species in water ballast. Steps are now being taken to curb this. Some believe that this exotic invasion is a more difficult problem than pollution was in the 1960s.

- Common fish species, such as rainbow smelt, alewife, white perch and common carp have all been introduced from outside, and non-native fish such as rainbow trout and brown trout continue to be stocked for anglers to catch, with results that are hard to quantify. The Great Lakes ecosystem, with its originally simple food chain, is fragile and highly vulnerable to invasion.

- Lake levels fluctuate, and are currently dropping.

- There is habitat loss from the shrinking of coastal wetlands that filter pollutants and provide fish spawning grounds.

- Global warming threatens more warmth and less precipitation in the area, and will increase demands from other states for the diversion of water from the lakes.

All three candidates for the 2008 presidential election race acknowledged the urgent need to address global warming, restore the lakes, and ban water diversion from the area.

In May 2008 all eight states and the two Canadian provinces bordering the lakes agreed to the Great Lakes Compact, establishing who can take water out of the lakes. The coalition is pushing Congress to adopt the compact and provide a $20 billion package for the conservation of the lakes.

The lakes are alive, and never more subject to watchful scrutiny or better protected by activists.

How to catch flying fish

Courtesy of the Barbados Ministry of Agriculture and Rural Development: "Fishing methods and gear used in Barbadian fisheries"

At the flying-fish ground the engine of the boat is turned off and the vessel allowed to drift. Bundles of cane trash, locally known as "screelers", are tied along a line at approximately 200-400-metre intervals. As the boat drifts, the line of screelers is released into the sea and allowed to float on the surface. A bait basket containing small pieces of fish (chum) is then hung over the side of the boat. The basket is shaken frequently either by the fishermen or as the boat rides the swells. These actions release small pieces of bait into the water. When enough flying fish reach the area a gill net is lowered into the water and is extended as the fishing boat continues to drift. The screelers are slowly pulled in and positioned in the vicinity of the net. When the flying fish circulating around the screeler try to pass through the almost unnoticeable net, they become entangled in the mesh; usually the fish's head passes through the mesh, but the rest of its body cannot. The frantic swimming action of the fish usually causes the netting to slip under the operculum (the hard protective flap covering the gills) of the fish, thus securely holding the fish.

How far can a flying fish fly?

In May 2008 a Japanese camera team filmed the longest flight of a flying fish ever recorded. Spotted off the southern tip of Japan, the fish sustained its flight for 45 seconds, beating the impressive 42 seconds registered by an American researcher in the 1920s. It kept up with a ferry, which was itself travelling at 20 mph, and it was able to continue flying by beating the surface of the water occasionally with its tail. Japanese experts say 45 seconds must be close to the physical limits of the animal, as brachial respiration is impossible while moving through the air.

Women and fish (I)

Records held by women anglers

Sarah Halley
In 1955, caught the biggest barracuda
ever landed up to that date: 66 lbs.

Lillian Scott
Hooked a massive goliath grouper in 1980: 454 lbs.

Maria Thomani
Landed a blue marlin in 1994: 950 lbs.

These are all world records, not just the best results achieved by women. And then there are the various national records, like the

British one achieved by **Georgina Ballantyne** in 1922, for a salmon weighing in at 64 lbs.

Clementine Morison achieved great success in fly fishing, traditionally a male preserve, when she caught a massive salmon in 1922. Unfortunately, there were no suitable scales on hand to weigh her catch until the next day, by which time it had already lost about two pounds in weight. However, it still managed an impressive 61 lbs.

Women and fish (II)

~

Why do women catch the biggest fish?

"When women fish, they do what the fishing guide tells them. Men think they know better. That's why with couples it's always the women who catch bigger fish."

— Galand Haas, fishing guide, Oregon

"Once women have a rod in their hands, they never let go of it. They are relentless."

—Hugh Falkus, British fly-fishing expert

The Eel

~

I don't mind eels
Except as meals.
And the way they feels

—*Ogden Nash*

The Eel Poem

~

When a dirty great eel
Makes you shudder and squirm
That's a moray

—*Peter Goulding*

The Octopus

~

Tell me, O Octopus, I begs
Is those things arms, or is they legs?
I marvel at thee, Octopus;
If I were thou, I'd call me Us.

—*Ogden Nash*

Youth is a shellfish age

~

"The world is your oyster, but your future's a clam"
—*Paul Weller*, lyric of "When You're Young", by The Jam

The king and the pie

On 24 February 1500, a child was born to Joanna the Mad and Philip the Fair of Spain: they christened him Charles. Thanks to the energetic bribing of some prince electors by the Fugger banking house, at the age of just nineteen Charles was elected as Holy Roman Emperor, becoming Charles V.

Charles was King of Spain, Sicily, Jerusalem, the Canary Islands and the Indies as well as the lands beyond the seas, Archduke of Austria, Duke of Burgundy, Brabant, Styria, Carinthia, Carniola, Luxemburg, Limburg, Athens and Neopatria, Count of Hapsburg, Flanders, Tyrol, Count in Swabia, Lord in Asia and Africa. The sun never set on his empire. Charles fought many wars against Italy and the Turks, and struggled with Luther and the rebellious peasants.

The Hapsburg Emperor had a poor command of German: "I speak Spanish to God, Italian to women, French to men, and German to my horse." He was said to be ugly, taciturn, and shy; he loved pocket watches and fatty food.

Charles abdicated in 1556, and retired to the remote Spanish monastery of Yuste, where he indulged his gluttonous appetite, especially for cold beer, anchovies, sausages, and eels. "Fish of every kind was to his taste, as, indeed, was anything that in its nature or habits at all approached to fish," says the American historian W. H. Prescott: "Eels, frogs, oysters occupied an important place in the royal bill of fare. Potted fish, especially anchovies, found great favour with him; and he regretted that he had not brought a better supply of these from the Low Countries. On an eel-pasty he particularly doted." In 1558 he ate a bad eel pie, and in three weeks the Emperor Charles was dead.

NB: English-language sources tend to say he died of fish poisoning; German ones favour a nervous collapse; and the Spanish versions cite malaria as the cause of death.

Straight from the horse's mouth

"'S'pose we take a look,' the longshoreman said over and over as he continued to haul in the line, now with increasing effort. He clambered down the stones toward the end of the line and stretched out both arms into the foaming pond between the granite blocks, clutched something—Mama turned away but not soon enough—he clutched something, changed his hold, tugged and heaved, shouted at them to make way, and flung something heavy and dripping, a great living lump of something down in our midst: it was horse's head, a fresh and genuine horse's head, the head of a black horse with a black mane, which only yesterday or the day before had no doubt been neighing; for the head was not putrid, it didn't stink, or if it did, then only of Mottlau water; but everything on the breakwater stank of that.

"The man in the longshoreman's cap—which had slipped down over the back of his neck—stood firmly planted over the lump of horsemeat, from which small light-green eels were darting furiously. The man had trouble in catching them, for eels move quickly and deftly, especially over smooth wet stones. Already the gulls were screaming overhead. They wheeled down, three or four of them would seize a small or medium-sized eel, and they refused to be driven away, for the breakwater was their domain. Nevertheless the longshoreman, thrashing and snatching among the gulls, managed to cram a couple of dozen small eels into the sack which Matzerath, who liked to be helpful, held ready for him. Matzerath was too busy to see Mama turn green and support first her hand, then her head, on Jan's shoulder and velvet collar."

—Günter Grass, *The Tin Drum*,
translated by Ralph Manheim

"The Great Tide Pool ... is a fabulous place. The sea is very clear and the bottom becomes fantastic with hurrying, fighting, breeding animals. Crabs rush from frond to frond of the waving algae. Starfish squat over mussels and limpets, attach their million little suckers and then slowly lift with incredible power until the prey is broken from the rock. And then the starfish stomach comes out and envelops its food. Orange and speckled and fluted nudibranchs slide gracefully over the rocks, their skirts waving like the dresses of Spanish dancers. And black eels poke their heads out of crevices and wait for prey. The lovely, colored world is glassed over. Hermit crabs like frantic children scamper on the bottom sand. And now one, finding an empty snail shell he likes better than his own, creeps out, exposing his soft body to the enemy for a moment, and then pops into the new shell ... Here a crab tears a leg from his brother. The anemones expand like soft and brilliant flowers, inviting any tired and perplexed animal to lie for a moment in their arms, and when some small crab or little tide-pool Johnnie accepts the green and purple invitation, the petals whip in, the stinging shells shoot tiny narcotic needles into the prey and it grows weak and perhaps sleepy while the searing caustic digestive acids melt its body down.

"Then the creeping murderer, the octopus, steals out, slowly, softly, moving like a gray mist, pretending now to be a bit of weed, now a rock, now a lump of decaying meat, while its evil goat eyes watch coldly. It oozes and flows toward a feeding crab, and as it comes close its yellow eyes burn and its body turns rosy with the pulsing color of anticipation and rage. Then suddenly it runs lightly on the tip of its arms, as ferociously as a charging cat. It leaps savagely on the crab, there is a puff of black fluid, and the struggling mass is obscured in the sepia cloud while the octopus murders the crab."

—John Steinbeck, *Cannery Row*

The joys of fishing

〜

O to have been brought up on bays, lagoons, creeks,
    or along the coast!
O to continue to be employ'd there all my life!
O the briny and damp smell—the shore—
    the salt weeds exposed at low water,
The work of fishermen—the work of the eel-fisher
    and clam-fisher.

—Walt Whitman, *Leaves of Grass*

Don't bother

〜

The first cookbook we can date exactly is that of "Platina",
i.e. Bartolomeo Sacchi, in 1472. He includes an eel-pie recipe,
only to give it a very low approval rating:

Eels in a Torta

To boiled eels that have been cut into bits, add either milk from
other fish or finely chopped soft fat. Cut up a little mint and parsley. Add an ounce of pine kernels, a like amount of raisins, a little
cinnamon, ginger, pepper, clove, and mix. Then spread it into your
crust. You should add a little best oil. When it is nearly cooked, dis-
solve two ounces of ground almonds in verjuice with saffron and
pass through a strainer and gently spread this over the whole top.
Palladius Rutilius is marvellously fond of this dish, even though it
is not good.

—From *Platina*, whose chapters on cookery in *De honesta
voluptate et valetudine* (*On Right Pleasure and Good Health*) drew
heavily on "the first modern cookbook", Maestro Martino's *The Art
of Cooking* (1450-1460), the earliest to give precise ingredients.

The oldest cookbook in English

The Forme of Cury (the art of cooking) is a 700-year-old scroll written during the reign of Richard II of England and composed of recipes created by the King's master cooks—highly paid and important officials. The roll was later presented to Queen Elizabeth I by Edward Lord Stafford. It includes a recipe for beaver, conveniently reclassified as a fish by the Church to skirt around the ban on meat-eating that applied to 242 days of the year. According to some of those who have tried them, one or two recipes are not very palatable today—for example, the "aigre-doux" (bitter-sweet, or sweet and sour) of fish topped with a kind of mulled vinegar. Many fish we do eat now do not appear among the recipes—there are no references to trout, flounders, herring, etc. But the seafood menu did include "porpoise in broth", as well as seal meat. One of Richard's feasts cost the equivalent of £70,000 for food and £12,000 for table linen.

Freud and the eel

⁓

"You know the eel. For a long time it was only the female of this beast that was known, Aristotle did not know where they got their mates from, and therefore had it that eels are formed from mud … Recently a Trieste zoologist claimed to have found the testicles of the eel, and thus the male of the species, but since he doesn't seem to know what a microscope is he did not provide a precise description. I am now tormenting myself and the eels looking for his male, but all the eels I dissect belong to the gentle sex."

—Sigmund Freud to his friend Eduard Silberstein

In 1876 Sigmund Freud was in the fifth semester of his medical studies when his professor, Karl Claus, packed him off to the Adriatic port of Trieste to work on the perennial eel question: were eels hermaphrodites? Where were the testicles? Where was the sperm? This was a hot topic. In Trieste, Freud dissected over 400 eels. He describes taking his evening walk at 6.30: "My hands stained from the white and red blood of the sea creatures, and in front of my eyes the glimmering debris of cells, which constantly disturbs me in my dreams, and in my mind nothing but the big problems connected with the names of testicles and ovaries—universally significant names."

It was all in vain. In his final report Freud had to admit defeat: "Histological investigation of the lobe-shaped organ does not allow me definitely to share the opinion that this is the eel's testicles, nor give me well-founded reasons for refuting it."

In fact, the sex of young eels is indeterminate. It is only just before they leave inland waters that the whole animal changes: their colour is altered, their nutrient intake becomes limited, the alimentary tract and the sexual organs develop. And it is only when they reach the Sargasso Sea, a long, long way from Trieste or Vienna, that they begin to produce sperm.

And now for some of the older theories

Izaak Walton on where eels come from

"It is agreed by most men, that the Eele is both a good and a most daintie fish; but most men differ about his breeding; some say, they breed by generation as other fish do; and others, that they breed (as some worms do) out of the putrifaction of the earth, and divers other waies; those that denie them to breed by generation, as other fish do, ask, if any man ever saw an Eel to have Spawn or Melt? And they are answered, That they may be as certain of their breeding, as if they had seen Spawn; for they say, that they are certain that Eeles have all parts fit for generation, like other fish, but so smal as not to be easily discerned, by reason of their fatness; but that discerned they may be; and that the Hee and the She Eele may be distinguished by their fins.

"And others say, that Eeles growing old, breed other Eeles out of the corruption of their own age, which Sir Francis Bacon sayes, exceeds not ten years. And others say, that Eeles are bred of a particular dew falling in the Months of May or June on the banks of some particular Ponds or Rivers (apted by nature for that end) which in a few dayes is by the Suns heat turned into Eeles …"

And so on and so forth

(Izaak Walton, The Compleat Angler, *1653)*

Izaak Walton is still the most famous writer in English on the subject of angling. Incidentally, the Chicago-based Izaak Walton League of America—founded in 1922 and one of the nation's oldest and most respected conservation organizations—has come to the rescue of Izaak Walton's cottage, now a museum in the UK, in Shallowford near Stone, Staffordshire. On account of the cost of upkeep, it was scheduled for closure. But by May 2008 an endowment from a brand new chapter of the League, the Izaak Walton Cottage Chapter, had helped to secure its future.

Electric eels and the life force

"In South America, electric eels prey on horses. These specimens of 'gymnotus' are 5-6 feet long. They are powerful enough to kill the strongest animal, if they manage to discharge all of their nerve-rich organs in the same moment at a favourable point. This is the wondrous battle of fish and horses. The unseen and living weapon of these aquatic animals is what is awakened by the contact of damp and dissimilar parts, what circulates in all the organs of animals and plants, what sets the wide sky alight to the sound of thunder, what binds iron to iron and directs the quiet, ceaseless movement of the compass needle; everything, like the colour of a ray of light when split, flows from one source, everything merges in one eternal, all-inclusive force."

—Alexander von Humboldt, *Aspects of Nature*, 1808

The ants of the ocean and the kibble of the sea

In the 8th and 9th centuries only coastal dwellers ate fish in northern Europe. This changed around the millennium, when people in the Baltic area discovered how to pickle herrings. Herrings are very fatty, which is why they are not as easy as cod to dry and smoke. The latter was caught further north, where spring is windy and sunny, ideal for stockfish (air-dried white fish). But salt herrings conquered the hinterland, and a whole industry sprang up on the Atlantic, North Sea and Baltic coasts. The Vikings invaded the Bay of Biscay to get access to the French salt fields, and Pope Alexander III lifted the ban on Sunday fishing. Herring was the new mass commodity of the Middle Ages. Not that it made the peasants' daily bread particularly tasty, because herring-pickling techniques still had a long way to go. In the 15th century the Hanseatic League with their characteristic broadly built "cog" boats dominated the herring trade, but then the herring disappeared: the Little Ice Age (1500 to 1850) had begun. The fishermen sought their fortunes ever further afield—discovering America in the process. Who knows whether it was Basque, Scandinavian or British fishing boats that first sailed to Newfoundland? The fishermen kept their route secret.

To this day, Atlantic herring are so prolific in the Gulf of Maine, for example, that counting the individual fish has been compared to "counting the ants in Portland, Maine", and the Atlantic herring vastly outnumbers other species. One member of the herring family, the small menhaden, makes up about 40% of the total commercial catch in the USA, and is used as animal foodstuff, known as "the kibble [dry pet food] of the sea". But, abundant as they are, menhaden are now being overfished. Spotter planes locate the huge shoals, which are then swept up wholesale by purse-seiner boats. All the large schools of menhaden in Rhode Island's Narragansett Bay have been destroyed. Not only are menhaden a vital part of the food chain for other fish, but along with oysters they are the most important filter feeders of inshore waters. They consume plankton, thereby removing a significant percentage of the excess nitrogen and phosphorus that cause the growth of algae. Without them, algal blooms proliferate, turning some inshore waters into dead zones.

Fish without end?

～

"The Herring shoal is a banquet at which the fish-eating sea crea-tures feed heartily, and man comes along, to spread his nets in the path of the shoal. But what matter a few million Herrings when the sea is packed with billions more! In the North Sea, one shoal was seen which was over four miles long and two miles wide. In such a mass there would be, at the very least, twenty thousand million Herring; and this shoal was but one out of many thousand shoals.

"Millions of Herrings are caught every year, forming a cheap and good food. Yet there are uncountable numbers left; and there is not the least danger that our nets can ever empty the sea of this wonderful little fish.

"It was thought, at one time, that the Whitebait was another kind of fish; but Whitebait are really the Herring and Sprat in their baby state."

—R. Cadwallader Smith, *Within the Deep* (1920s)

20 May 1789

～

From *A Narrative of the Mutiny on Board His Majesty's Ship Bounty* by William Bligh

Our distresses were now very great, and we were so covered with rain and salt water, that we could scarcely see ... and every one dreaded the approach of night. About two o'clock in the morning we were overwhelmed with a deluge of rain. It fell so heavy that we were afraid it would fill the boat ... At dawn of day, I served a large allowance of rum ... The usual allowance of one 25th of a pound of bread and water was served at evening, morning, and noon.

Whiskey compass

~

When the skipper feels thirsty, he looks longingly at his gyrocompass, for early compasses floated in alcohol. Is this still the case?

We examined various models:

Sperr-Brown single gyrocompass: no fluid in the compass, just mercury. Vibration damping
Anschütz single gyrocompass: no fluid. Mercury damping
Plath Navigat twin gyrocompass, spherical gyrocompass: small amounts of mercury in casing
Anschütz twin gyrocompass: a mixture of glycerine and water
Plath Standard VII: distilled water
Fibre-optic gyroscope: no fluid
Magnetic compass: denatured alcohol

Sweet and sour carp

~

Serves six

1 carp (4-5 lbs.)	Pork fat
1 egg	Canned tomatoes
4 shallots	Light soy sauce
1/2 cup sherry	Vinegar
2 pieces candied ginger	Stock
Ginger syrup	Sugar, white pepper, salt
Flour	

Trim the fins off the carp, descale, cut in half lengthways, and fillet. Divide into bite-sized chunks and run under cold water, allow to drain, then dry. Rub salt and pepper into the pieces of carp, place in a bowl and pour sherry over them. Allow 20 minutes to marinade.

Whisk the egg in a bowl. Sprinkle the flour on a plate, and coat the carp pieces with egg, then flour. Heat up a frying pan and fry the coated pieces for 15 minutes in two tablespoons of fat until golden brown, turning them over once.

For the sauce, cube the shallots and fry them golden brown in a tablespoon of fat. Cut the ginger into strips and add them to the shallots with the syrup.

Use a small saucepan on a low heat to caramelize the sugar, add two tablespoons soy sauce, a tablespoon of vinegar, a tablespoon of tinned tomato and three tablespoons of stock to the sugar, then pour over the shallots. Boil up briefly with two tablespoons of water, finally season with salt and pepper. Arrange the pieces of fish on lettuce leaves and pour the sauce over them.

The people of Japan

They are a people who eat three times a day, and each time they eat very little. They eat very little meat, and as I have said they do not eat chicken. It seems to me the reason is that they rear them at home, and they do not eat what they rear. Their diet consists of rice and pulses, mung beans, millet, buckwheat, yam and wheat. They seem to eat the latter cooked to a porridge: I never saw them making bread. They drink arrack made from rice, and another drink that they all drink, young and old. I never saw anyone drunk out of their senses. As soon as they recognise that they have had enough, they take themselves off to bed. There are many inns and restaurants in the country, where you can eat and drink and stay overnight. They eat cheese made from beans which looks like [our] fresh cheese; I do not know how it tastes, for I have never tried it. They eat sitting on the floor like

Muslims, and with chopsticks like the Chinese. Everyone eats out of their own painted bowls, and from porcelain and wooden vessels, painted black on the outside and red inside, containing their food. In summer they drink hot barley water, and in winter water containing herbs, though we could not discover which herbs. They never drink cold water, neither in summer nor in winter."

This letter was written to Francis Xavier (1506-52, a founding member of the Jesuits, and posthumous protector of seafarers) in 1546 by the Portuguese merchant Jorge Alvares. For a long time Alvares was known as the best source of information about the reclusive island empire.

Varieties of sushi

FUNA: carp stored in salt for three years and stuffed with rice (the rice was not eaten)—Lake Biva, Japan, around 700 AD

AYU: a half-raw freshwater fish fermented under stones for a month (the rice was eaten)—Japan, around 1500

SABA: rice soured with vinegar with pressed fish—Japan, around 1600

TORO-NIGRI: red tuna, the dearest sushi fish—Tokyo, 1960s

CALIFORNIA ROLL: cucumber, avocado, surimi in a rice roll—Los Angeles, 1970s

RAINBOW ROLL: mango, avocado, surimi in a rice roll—Singapore, 1980s

SAMBA ROLL: eel, salmon, roast prawns in a rice roll—Brazil, 1990s

POTATO SUSHI: potatoes instead of rice—Frankfurt am Main, 2004

WHITE SAUSAGE SUSHI: white sausage on rice mixed with sweet mustard—Berlin, 2007 (© Lorenz Schröter, the author of this book)

Puffer fish for beginners

~

The best-known
representative of its kind
is the fugu: a minute dose of its
muscle-paralysing poison tetrodotoxin
(TTX) is enough to cause death through respiratory
standstill while still fully conscious. It is true that puffer
fish can now be bred without their poison, but then this
expensive dish loses its appeal. Gourmets
love the prickly, numbing sensation on
their lips and tongue of takifugu
rubripes when there is still
a trace of poison

Fugu à la carte

~

FUGU SUSHI: sashimi, raw, and so thin as to be transparent, often made into the shape of a crane or a chrysanthemum

HIRE-ZAKE: grilled, dried fugu fins in hot sake

FUGUCHIRI: stew with fugu and vegetables. A droplet from the liver, the most poisonous part of the fish, gives the dish that little extra.

YUBIKI: salad made with fugu skin

Table manners when eating fugu

~

- The chef is boss. Listen to the cook and follow his instructions!
- Do not drum with your chopsticks.
- Do not make faces or silly jokes about the fish.
- Do not let others have a taste, feed them or share with them.
- Do not smoke.
- Do not turn pale when the bill arrives. (Incidentally, you don't normally tip in Japan.)

Deaths caused by fugu since 1886

~

6,925
And about 50 more are added every year—most of the victims being fishermen who eat their own catch.

Death haiku

~

I am not seeing her today
I shall give her up
And eat fugu

—Yosa Buson (1716-1783)

Fugu restaurants outside Japan

Nippon ≈ 155 East 52nd Street, New York
Soba Nippon ≈ 19 West 52nd Street, New York
Yodo ≈ 13 East 47th Street, New York
Chikabu ≈ 12 East 44th Street, New York
Naniwa ≈ 4 East 46th Street, New York
Azusa ≈ 3 East 44th Street, New York
Nadaman Hakubai ≈ 66 Park Avenue, New York
Inagiku ≈ 111 East 49th Street, New York
Sugiyama Restaurant ≈ 251 West 55th Street, New York
Taiko ≈ 15 South Village Avenue, Rockville Centre, New York
Bond Street ≈ 6 Bond Street, New York
Hatsuhana Restaurant ≈ 17 East 49th Street, New York
Kaz Sushi Bistro ≈ 1915 I Street, NW, Washington, DC
New Otani LA ≈ 120 South Los Angeles Street, Los Angeles
Morimoto Restaurant ≈ 723 Chestnut Street, Philadelphia
Tako Grill ≈ 7756 Wisconsin Avenue, Bethesda, Maryland
Shiki Restaurant ≈ 4 Westroy Street, Seattle

Fugu and the zombies

Voodoo is an African religion with followers in West Africa and the Caribbean. European and American culture is particularly fascinated by the image of the zombie. George Romero's film *Night of the Living Dead* is an obvious case in point: it can be seen as a cinematic equivalent of Dante's *Inferno*. A whole interpretation industry has accrued around this film classic. Of course, this has nothing to do with the religious origins of the zombie.

The Canadian Wade Davis thinks he has discovered the causes of "zombification": poison from the puffer fish. Tetrodotoxin (TTX) is a very strong nerve toxin, and has been found in all effective zombie powders. Davis also detected traces of poison from the cane toad (bufo marinus) and the Hispaniola tree frog (osteopilus dominicensis). TTX paralyses its victims: although conscious, they cannot move or speak—they become zombies. They are to all appearances dead, and are buried accordingly, fully conscious, only to be "raised from the dead" three days later by the houngan (Voodoo priest). But only in Haiti.

Famous victims of fish
~

Henry I of England, 1135
Cause of death: "A surfeit of lampreys" (eel-like fish)—though nowadays fish poisoning thought the more likely cause

Charles V, Holy Roman Emperor, 1558
Cause of death: Eel pie

Ed Morris, Boston Red Sox pitcher, 1932
Cause of death: Stabbed to death when he tried to break up a fight at a fish fry given in his honour in Century, Florida.

Bando Mitsugoro VIII, Kabuki star, 1975
Cause of death: Fugu

Daphne Zuniga, "Jo Reynolds" in drama serial *Melrose Place* set in Los Angeles, 2005; just barely survived
Cause: Tuna and sushi 5 times a week led to mercury poisoning

Steve Irwin, the Crocodile Hunter, 2006
Cause: Chest pierced by barb of a stingray

Giant squid

It is hard to connect the small sea creatures we enjoy as calamari with the monster squid that was recently dissected at a New Zealand museum—one of only about ten of these giants ever to have been brought to shore. Measuring around 33 feet across, they live at great sea depths, and to utilize what light there is on the ocean floor they have the largest eyes on earth—about a foot in diameter. Being related to the octopus, which is known to have a very good memory, they are thought to be quite intelligent. An uncomfortable thought when we are consuming their smaller cousins fried, with mayonnaise?

Here be monsters

It is often said that we know more about the surface of Mars than we do about the depths of the oceans. "It is clear from measuring the sucker marks on dead whales that immense battles must take place in the middle deeps involving squid of a size never yet seen … The great mass of the oceans remains unexplored, even as the contours of their beds are electronically surveyed. Their waters must hide many species strange to taxonomy," says James Hamilton-Paterson, in *Seven-Tenths: The Sea and its Thresholds*. There are many historical accounts of sea-monster sightings, some of them from impeccable sources. Nick Redfern, the British expert on paranormal events and UFOs who settled in the USA in 2001, recently told listeners to the American broadcasting channel

"Uncanny Radio" about material he had unearthed in the Public Records Office in Kew, London, including this report based on a ship's logbook, than which nothing could be more sober:

"Let me quote to you the text of one such report, written in 1830 by Captain James Stockdale of the ship the *Rob Roy*, who had an amazing encounter near the island of St. Helena on Sunday, May 9 of that year. Stockdale wrote: 'About five p.m. all at once while I was walking on the poop my attention was drawn to the water on the port bow by a scuffling noise. Judge my amazement when what should stare us all in the face as if not knowing whether to come over the deck or to go around the stern—but the great thundering big sea snake! My ship is 171 feet long overall—and the foremast is 42 feet from the stern which would make the monster about 129 feet long. The brute was so close I could even smell his nasty fishy smell.' This is just a small extract from Stockdale's account and it makes for bizarre and illuminating reading. And this is just one of a number of such accounts held in the British Admiralty's Sea Serpent File."

Redfern may regularly be heard in person talking at the Massachusetts Monster Mash (the venue for 2009 was Watertown, MA). The cryptozoologist Michael A. Woodley, following up the 1950s work of the respected researcher Heuvelmans, has produced the definitive study, *In the Wake of Bernard Heuvelmans: An Introduction to the History and Future of Sea Serpent Classification*. His scholarly, scientific conclusion is that these sea-monsters really do exist. In Devon there is a Centre for Fortean Zoology set up by John Downes to study monsters of the deep and giant fish.

Monster mice

In the South Atlantic, mice that came ashore from whaling ships 150 years ago have evolved to THREE TIMES the size of ordinary house mice. On British-owned Gough Island, without any natural predators, their numbers have reached 700,000. The island hosts the most important seabird population in the world, with twenty-two breeding species, and is a world heritage site. Disturbingly, instead of living off insects and seeds, the mice have turned carnivorous, eating albatross, petrel and shearwater chicks alive in their nests. The Gough bunting, which only exists on the island, is critically endangered; five other bird species are also threatened. Sixty per cent of all Gough's birds are dying in their nests. There is a way to save them. Elsewhere (including in the UK), such pests have been dealt with by dropping rodent poison. To apply this remedy to the volcanic island 2,000 miles from the coast of South America would cost an estimated $5.2 million. Unfortunately, Britain does not have a good reputation when it comes to protecting the ecology of its overseas island possessions. The British are now officially responsible for thirty-two of the 190 most endangered birds in the world.

The *Mayflower*

~

*C*ontrary to popular belief, Southampton was the port from which the Pilgrim Fathers (not so called until 1799) set out to cross the Atlantic, and not Plymouth, which was never on their itinerary. It was in Southampton that they provisioned their ship, along with the *Speedwell*, and prepared the two vessels for the voyage. They put in at Plymouth, Devon, only because the *Speedwell* sprang a leak, and had to be left behind there. The fact that they landed in North America near a place called Plymouth was probably a coincidence. It was not named by the pilgrims, but by Captain John Smith (of Pocahontas fame), who had explored the coastline in 1614; the name was taken from the Plymouth Virginia Company, granted a charter to colonize by King James I in 1606. In Southampton today there is a Mayflower Park, a Mayflower Theatre, and the fine Mayflower monument erected in 1913: a column topped by a copper replica of the ship, and bearing a plaque which commemorates both the pilgrims and the two million US troops who embarked from Southampton more than 300 years later, during World War II. If you can prove an ancestral connection with the pilgrims, you can have a plaque added to the memorial. Southampton certainly has not forgotten its connection with the settlers.

Caviar: the luxury we have

~

"Caviar is a luxury we have. Time is not."
—Bob Hoskins as Nikita Khrushchev
in the movie *Enemy at the Gate* 2001

—Price per kilo—

Beluga: Charcoal-grey, large and firm-grained, skin
  extremely thin, very mild, $6,677 (£4,084) (from
  Amazon.com).

Almas: Ivory-coloured caviar from the albino beluga.
  Used to be reserved exclusively for the Tsar. Persian
  Almas is sold in 24-carat gold jars, $69,267 (£42,363)
  (from Caviar House & Prunier, London).

Ossietra: Silvery-grey to black, faint golden sheen, tougher
  skin, nutty. Royal Black is a deep black, young Ossietra.
  Imperial, golden brown Ossietra with bright sheen,
  $3,078 (£1,882) (from Desietta in Fulda, Germany).

Keluga: Black, from China, $2,309 (£1,412).

Sevruga: Grey, quite large, thin skin, delicate; strong and
  spicy flavour. In a glass jar with a red or orange lid,
  $3,060 (£1,871) (from Amazon.com).

Caviar to the general: roe that isn't sturgeon

"The play, I remember, pleas'd not the million, 'twas caviare to the general" —Hamlet

Keta-caviar: Pacific salmon roe

Perles du Nord: lumpfish

Limfjord caviar: lumpfish

German caviar: lumpfish

Bottarga, Sicilian caviar: tuna

Sikröm: white fish (orfe, bream, chub, carp, white bream, dace, white aspe, bleak, zobel, zope, bluenose)

Kalixlöjro: vendace

Capelin: capelin (related to the smelt)

Löjrom: herring

Masago, tobbiko: flying fish

Tarama: carp

Tarako: cod

Also tasty: roe of the trout and whitefish

Beyond price

Imraguen mullet botarga is a Mauretanian caviar confined to the Banc d'Arguin national park, where nomads with motor-less boats are the only people allowed to fish. The Imraguen women salt, rinse and press mullet eggs between boards after passing schools of dolphin have steered the fish, undamaged by trawling, towards their nets.

From Abba to zander

～

The Swedish firm Abba have been selling fish in cans since 1838. In 1969, when Agneta, Björn, Benny and Anna-Frida wanted to name their band after their initials, the fish-canners gave their permission, as long as it brought no disrepute to their brand products (Fisbullar, Kosttillskott, Sillinäggningar).

What did Francis Drake do for the US?

～

During his voyage round the world, Drake sailed further north along the west coast of North America than any other European before him. On 17 June 1579 he landed in what is now California, somewhere north of Spain's most northerly claim at Point Loma. (It is also thought that he sailed much further north, to land also at Whale Cove, Oregon, or Comox on Vancouver Island. His route was kept secret by order of Queen Elizabeth, for fear of conceding too much information to the Spaniards. The records were later burnt in Whitehall Palace.) In California he is traditionally said to have landed—as the name suggests—at Drake's Bay in Marin County, a claim supposedly reinforced by the modern discovery of "Drake's Plate of Brass", a plaque which turned out to be a hoax. New calculations based on Drake's navigation calculations now seem to show that he landed anywhere from Bodega to San Pablo Bay.

What matters is that Drake claimed the new land for his queen, calling it "Nova Albion" (New England), and maps made soon after showed "Nova Albion" inscribed above the entire northern frontier of New Spain. In the 1600s, all colonial claims made from the east coast were "from sea to sea". These claims were based on full awareness of Drake's assertions of English sovereignty. When the colonies achieved independence, Drake's claims remained valid in the minds of the ex-colonialists, and they became very important during the negotiations that ended the Mexican-American War.

A long shelf life—thanks to the sun

In prehistoric times hunter-gatherers air-dried herbs and grasses, seeds and meat. Removing water prevents growth and stops the process of decomposition. This was particularly successful with seeds like that of single-grain spelt. It did not take long to find out that these grains could be planted and harvested. People could now decide whether they wanted to settle and harvest crops, or go on hunting and gathering—and go hungry in winter. It was the Egyptians who eventually baked the first flat bread, an art that was soon picked up by others, including the Jews. That is why bread is mentioned so often in the Bible. In a separate development, for about 4,000 years the Chinese have been rolling dough out thin, cutting it into strips, and drying it as noodles.

A long shelf life—thanks to salt

Aristophanes was already referring to salted fish in his first comedy, *The Acharnians* (425 BC). The Romans seem to have used salt first and foremost for pickling; their main relish, garum liquarem, was a salty fish sauce. The word "sausage" is derived from the Latin salsicia (salted food). This oldest addition to foodstuffs removes water from meat and fish, thereby depriving harmful organisms, germs and infections of a medium in which to grow.

The Vikings were only able to undertake their long voyages because of salted and smoked provisions—they could not cook in their open wooden ships.

29 May 1789

From *A Narrative of the Mutiny on Board His Majesty's Ship Bounty* by William Bligh

*A*s we advanced within the reefs … in our way towards the shore I came to a grapnel, and tried to catch fish, but had no success … I found a bay and a fine sandy point to land at … Every one was anxious to find something to eat, and I soon heard that there were oysters on the rocks, for the tide was out; but it was nearly dark, and only a few could be gathered.

Boston Tea Party

16 December 1773: 90,000 lbs. (45 tons) of tea worth $1.87 million (£1.14 million) in today's money were tipped into Boston Harbor. The Americans were smuggling in tea from Holland instead of accepting consignments from the British East India Company, which officially had a monopoly of the tea trade between India and the British colonies. The East India Company was close to bankruptcy because of all the unsold tea piling up in its warehouses. It was prepared to sell its tea without imposing a tax. However, the American smugglers faced being put out of business by this cheaper British tea, as they did not trust their fellow colonists to be patriotic enough not to buy it. They staged further tea parties in New Hampshire, New York City, Elizabethstown (now Hagerstown) and Weston. As we know, it was the beginning of the American Revolution.

But the burning question remains: what kind of tea was it? Contemporary sources refer to Bohea, black tea from the Wuyi Mountains area of China. However, most school textbooks cite Darjeeling—which was not cultivated for another century, and came from India, not China.

Boston Tea Party: "I was there!'

112 participants are listed below—some with really fine names

Moses Axtell · Nathaniel Barber · Samuel Barnard · Henry Bass · Edward Bates · Thomas Boulter · David Bradlee · James Bradlee · Thomas Bradlee · James Brewer · John Brown · Stephen Bruce · Benjamin Burton · Nicholas Campbell · George Carleton · Thomas Chase · Benjamin Clarke · John Cochran · Nathaniel Coleman · Gresham Collier · Adam Colson · James F. Condy · S. Coolidge · Samuel Cooper · Thomas Crafts Jr. · John Crane · Thomas Dana · Robert Davis · John Dickerman · Edward Dolbear · Joseph Eaton · Joseph Eayres · Benjamin Edes · William Etheridge · Samuel Fenno · Samuel Foster · Nathaniel Frothingham · John Fulton · John Gammell · Samuel Gore · Moses Grant · John Greenleaf · Samuel Hammond · William Hendley · George R. Hewes · John Hicks · Samuel Hobbs · John Hooton · Samuel Howard · Edward C. Howe · Jonathan Hunnewell · Richard Hunnewell · Richard Hunnewell Jr. · Thomas Hunstable · Abraham Hunt · David Ingersoll · Seth Ingersoll · David Kennison · Joseph Lee · Amos Lincoln · Mathew Loring · Joseph Lovering · Thomas Machin · Ebenezer MacKintoch · Archibald McNeil · John May · Thomas Melvill · William Molineux · Thomas Moore · Anthiny Morse · Joseph Montford · Eliphalet Newell · Joseph P. Palmer · Jonathan Parker · Joseph Payson · Samuel Peck · John Peters · William Pierce · Lendall Pitts · Thomas Potter ·Henry Prentiss · John Prince · Edward Proctor · Henry Purkitt · John Randall · Paul Revere · Joseph Roby · John Russell · William Russell · Robert Sessions · Joseph Shed · Benjamin Simpson · Peter Slater · Samuel Spraque · John Spurr · James Starr · Phineas Stearns · Ebenezer Stevens · Elisha Story · James Swan · John Truman · Thomas Urann · Peter Watertown · Josiah Wheeler · David Williams · Isaac Williams · Jeremiah Williams · Thomas Williams · Nathaniel Willis · Joshua Winslow · Joshua Wyeth · Thomas Young

A long shelf life—thanks to freezing

Francis Bacon's carriage ran over a chicken in the winter of 1626. He stuffed it with snow and ate it at home later. And so frozen food was born. Sadly, Bacon caught a chill in the process and developed pneumonia, from which he died not long afterwards.

Carl von Linde developed the first freezer machine in 1876. Just a year later, the first frozen beef carcases were being shipped from the Argentine to France.

The marine biologist Clarence Birdseye was a dealer in furs from 1812 to 1816, and saw the Canadian Inuit fast-freezing meat. He invented a method of doing the same thing in warmer climes, and on 6 March 1830 the housewives of Springfield, Massachusetts were able for the first time to buy frozen food in the supermarket. In 1854 Birdseye also invented a way of freezing freshly caught fish on board trawlers.

In 2004 Bird's Eye decided to ditch its famous seagull logo in favour of a tear-shaped emblem in red and yellow "to bring an element of natural-ness and warmth [!] to the products", as a spokeswoman said. Perhaps the switch had something to do with the "nosediving" (in both senses) reputation of seagulls. Gulls have certainly had a bad press in the seaside town of Brighton, where they frequently steal food, especially tuna sandwiches, from under people's noses at outdoor cafés. They closed a school for a day by their aggressive defence of newly hatched chicks in a nest on the school roof. In other shocking incidents, one seagull landed on a youth's head and snatched a burger out of his hand; another bird made off with a senior citizen's false teeth, which were lying on a garden table; and a man living in a Brighton attic was woken up by the noise of a seagull banging a flatfish against his skylight to finish it off. Brighton and Hove Albion football team are known as the Seagulls.

Reefers, refrigerator cars, and the "Red Man"

The first refrigerator ship, using natural ice, was in use by 1856, but by the 1870s ships with artificial refrigeration, quickly abbreviated to "reefers", were beginning to carry meat and other produce across the world from Australia, New Zealand and South America. The era of cheap food had arrived. In a few years, the annual export of American beef to the British Isles rose from 109,500 pounds to 72 million pounds. "Out of season" fruit was no longer just a luxury for royals.

Within the United States, refrigeration was as important an element in the expansion and growth of cities as the railroad, lifts and telecommunications were. The authorities in San Francisco, for example, decided to bulk out the numbers of West Coast clams by bringing a refrigerator carload of clams from the eastern seaboard to San Francisco Bay—the beginnings of a new industry there. Refrigerator cars and refrigerated storage meant that meat from the American West could be shipped east, and the enormous demand for meat led to ranchers and the federal government taking over millions of acres, driving the buffalo to near extinction—and with it the "Red Man" whose way of life was based on buffalo. So it wasn't only the iron horse that displaced Native Americans; it was also the refrigerator.

The fish trade

Fish and fishery products are the most internationally traded food-stuffs in the world. About 38 per cent of the world fish by live weight is traded internationally. In values terms, 50 per cent of the trade originates in developing countries, while almost 80 per cent of fish imports are destined for the US, EU, and Japan markets.

(As reported by GLOBEFISH, the databank unit based in the Fisheries Department of the UN Food and Agriculture Organization, usually abbreviated to FAO.)

You couldn't make it up … or could you?

In July 2006, fish up to 2.2 inches long rained down for about a quarter of an hour upon the Indian village of Manna, in Kerala. It is thought that the pencil-thin fish were probably lifted into the sky by a waterspout, or a mini-tornado. Not all that falls from the sky is manna from heaven, however: Pliny the Elder in his *Naturalis Historiae* reports that "in the consulship of L. Paulus and C. Marcellus it rained wool, round the castle of Carissanum, near which place, a year after, T. Annius Mile was killed. It is recorded, among the transactions of that year, that when he was pleading his own cause, there was a shower of baked tiles."

Jellyfish salad

1/2 lb. dried jellyfish (available from Chinese emporia)
strips of green, yellow, and red peppers
sesame oil   chilli oil
1/2 lb. cucumber, cut into strips   soy sauce
5 morel mushrooms   vinegar
sugar

Rinse the jellyfish for twenty minutes under cold water, dry off and cut in strips. Blanch in boiling water without salt. Rinse with cold water. Put in a bowl with the paprika strips, cucumber, and morels. Make a sauce from the soy sauce, sugar, sesame oil and chilli oil.

Fishers of men

~

The first four of Jesus' disciples were fishermen: Simon Peter, his brother Andrew, James, and his brother John. It says in St Mark's gospel: "And Jesus said to them: Come after me; and I will make you to become fishers of men. And immediately leaving their nets, they followed him." Two of them, Peter and James, are associated with particular sea creatures:

St Peter's fish, St Pierre, or John Dory: flat-bodied, the spiny deep-sea fish swims across the floor of the eastern Atlantic. It is olive yellow in colour, and on its side is a large dark spot, often ringed with gold. Legend has it that this is the thumbprint left by St Peter when he drew a gold coin out of its mouth to pay his and Jesus' taxes.

Scallop of James the Greater: The scallop badge or emblem is traditionally worn by pilgrims on their way to the shrine of Santiago (St James) de Compostela in Spain. The story is told that when James's body was being taken by sea to Spain, a young knight riding out to meet it fell in the sea and was drowned. But he was miraculously brought back to life by the saintliness of James, and emerged from the water covered in scallops.

And then there is the "*Judas fish*". Anglers will stop at nothing to land their prey. If they catch a fish that normally swims in shoals or schools, they attach a kind of float to it and put it back in the water. When the fish rejoins the school, as it naturally will, the angler knows where to find rich pickings. The fish has betrayed the school.

Abalone

It goes under many names in various languages: Seeohr (meaning "sea-ear", German), paua (Maori, New Zealand), ormer (English, Channel Islands), ear shell, sea ear, Venus's shell (English), muttonfish, muttonshell (English, Australia) takobushi (Japanese), perlemoen (Afrikaans, South Africa), loco (Spanish, Chile), haliotis (Latin); but all the same it is not particularly well known. So it is worth taking a look at its family connections.

Abalone belongs to the molluscs, along with mussels, sea cucumbers and cephalopods (squid and octopus). Among these they are classified as marine snails, since they are univalves—i.e. they only have a one-piece shell (if you find a single-shell mussel on the beach, then it's a snail!).

Their meat is tasty and very dear. Trimmed, sliced, and pounded ready to cook, they cost from £18 to £42 a pound. Most often it is only the muscle flesh of the foot that is eaten, raw as sashimi or lightly steamed, in which case the flesh is pounded, or flattened beforehand with a broad knife blade. The gonad is also reckoned a delicacy in Japan. The nervous system of the abalone consists of four pairs of ganglions around the mouth, which enable it to balance so well. Transparent blood flows through its heart. Its foot muscle enables it to flee from its greatest predator (after humans), the starfish. Otherwise, it grazes peacefully on algae. Young abalones hide under sea urchins to escape detection.

Thousands of layers made up of individual tiles only a hundredth of the thickness of a human hair make the mother-of-pearl shell enormously hard. Materials scientists at the University of San Diego have constructed body armour along the same lines—it withstands sudden blows better than aluminium does.

Abalones are farmed all over the world, even in Iceland, and poached throughout the world (the first underwater arrest took place in Guernsey, when a policeman in full diving gear apprehended somebody illegally diving for abalone). The white abalone may soon become the first marine invertebrate to be driven to extinction by human activities.

Glass floats

A very, very long time ago, before styrofoam was invented and when cork was really dear, fisherman suspended their nets in the water from single glass balls, or bundles of balls tied together. This started in Norway with the thick brown globes made by Christian Berg's Hadelands Glassverk in Bergen. From there, the glass floats conquered the rest of Europe, North America, and in 1900 even Japan. Different balls were developed for every type of net, up to 20 inches in diameter, and in all colours.

These floats are still frequently washed up on shore. There are said to be millions of them drifting around the oceans.

There is nothing that is not collectable. The collectors' market for glass balls takes place on the first weekend in March every year at Beachcomber's Fun Fair, Ocean Shores, Washington. A genuine glass net float fetches up to $3,000 (£1,800) there. Originals are sorted out from replicas, and enthusiasts discuss the finer points of the *Collectors' Price Guide and Identification Handbook to Glass Fishing Floats of the World*, by Stu Farnsworth and Alan D. Rammer.

What exactly is a sea-bean?

Sea-beans (aka drift seeds) are seeds and fruits that drift down to the sea in freshwater streams and rivers, then float away on the ocean currents and fetch up on beaches.

Some are actually beans, but many are not; they may be fruit containing seeds. However, "sea-bean" is the term used by beach-combers for all such bounty from the ocean.

The first circumnavigation of the globe

"We left the straits behind us on Wednesday 28 November and entered an ocean where we sailed for three months and twenty days without enjoying a morsel of fresh food. The biscuit we ate was no longer biscuit, but dust mixed with weevils and mouse droppings, and it stank unbearably. The water that we were obliged to drink was also foul and evil-smelling. To fend off starvation, we ate the leather that was wrapped around the yard-arm to protect the ropes. These pieces of leather, constantly exposed to the water, sun and wind, were so hard that we had to soak them for four or five days in sea-water to soften them up. Then we spread them over coals and forced them down our throats, shivering with disgust. Often there was nothing left to eat but sawdust; and even mice, much as men abhor them, had become such sought-after food that they fetched up to half a ducat a piece. During these terrible days four of our number died, and as soon as anyone breathed his last Magellan had his body quickly committed to the deep. He was probably afraid that one or other of us would resort to cannibalism. I saw one man casting greedy eyes upon a dead Spaniard, grinding his lower jaw to and fro, and I had no doubt that this seaman was considering which piece he might cut from the corpse and swallow raw. Two bosuns got into an argument over a rat that had been caught, and one slew the other with the ax he had used to kill the rat. Magellan had him brought aboard our ship and condemned him to death. The bosun was sentenced to be quartered, but nobody had the strength to carry out the sentence. So he was strangled and his body thrown into the sea." —Antonio Pigafetta, *The First Circumnavigation of the Globe*, 1524.

Magellan, Pigafetta and two hundred and thirty-two other men set sail in five ships on 10 August 1519 from the river port of Seville on the first circumnavigation of the world. Their goal was the Spice Islands. After three years almost to the day, eighteen men and just one ship returned.

The Little Book of the Sea calendar

~

End of January
Thorinn, an ancient heathen festival in Iceland with "interesting" Viking dishes

Middle of February
Chilli Cooking Competition in Ajijic, Mexico

End of February
Canadian Ice Fishing Championship, Georgina, Ontario

March
At the Argungu Fish Festival in Nigeria up to three thousand fishermen try their luck, standing with hand-held nets in the river

April
Cherry blossom in Japan; picnicking in the park

Mid-April
Songkran in Chiang Mai—the Thai New Year festival is famous for its water fights, khantoke dinners, and cooking competitions ("khantoke" refers to the special low wooden table or pedestal trays on which five dishes plus boiled rice are served)

Second weekend in May
At the Sagra del Pesce in Camogli, Italy, large numbers of fish are deep-fried and handed out gratis

Last weekend in May
The new matjes herrings arrive in Holland

Last full week in June

Kieler Woche—"Kiel Week" claims to be the biggest sailing regatta in the world, held since 1882. However, Cowes Week in the Isle of Wight has been running since 1826 and also claims to be the "biggest regatta of its kind in the world". 30 nations are present in Kiel Week, bringing with them their culinary and cultural delights

Second weekend in July

Fish soup competition in Baja, Hungary

End of July

Singapore Food Festival

Early August

Lobster Festival in Maine; Cowes Week regatta, Isle of Wight, held on first Saturday after last Tuesday in July—tides permitting.

Second week in August

Hansa Sail in Rostock—windjammer rally with culinary delicacies

Third Thursday in August

The new surströmming (rotten fish) comes on the market in Sweden

Last weekend in September

World oyster-shucking speed contest in Galway, Ireland

Mid-October

Sea-bean Symposium and Beachcombers' Festival at Cocoa Beach, Florida—meeting for fans of flotsam and jetsam, messages in bottles, and ocean currents

Early November

Rum Festival in St Lucia, West Indies

December

The lutefisk (traditional fish dish of Nordic countries) season begins in Scandinavia and Minnesota

About the author

~

LORENZ SCHRÖTER was born in 1960, is a travel writer, and with his *Little Book of the Sea* wrote the best book in the world (according to the German publication *Zweite Hand Bootshandel*, ["Second-Hand Boat Trade"]). He spent two years cycling around the world, from Gibraltar to Africa, Asia and Central America and back. Then he lived for three years on a small traffic-free island off Hong Kong. Back in Europe, he travelled through Germany on a donkey. He has crossed the Straits of Hormuz in a dhow, travelled on a container ship from Singapore to Hong Kong, and has so far collected 110 country points according to the rules of the Travelers' Century Club. Lorenz Schröter has a home in Berlin, but feels at home all over the world.